STECK-VAUGHN

TABE® Language

Fundamentals

Focus on Skills

LEVEL E

Return to Michelle Hunt
Room 3

Steck Vaughn®

HOUGHTON MIFFLIN HARCOURT

www.SteckVaughn.com/AdultEd
800-289-4490

Reviewer

Jerry Birschbach
ABE/GED Instructor
Americana Learning Center
Jefferson County Public Schools—Adult Education
Louisville, Kentucky

Printed in the United States of America

ISBN 13: 978-0-547-29658-6
ISBN 10: 0-547-29658-4

5 6 7 8 9 1689 17 16 15 14 13 12

4500354449   C D E F G

Contents

To the Learner

You are taking an important step in your educational career by studying for the TABE. This book will help you do your best on the TABE. You'll also find hints and strategies that will help you prepare for test day. Practice these skills—your success lies in your hands.

What Is the TABE?

TABE stands for the Tests of Adult Basic Education. These paper-and-pencil tests, published by McGraw-Hill, measure your progress on basic skills. The tests get harder with each level because you continue to be tested on skills learned at earlier levels. There are seven tests in all: Reading, Mathematics Computation, Applied Mathematics, Language, Vocabulary, Language Mechanics, and Spelling.

TABE Levels E, M, D, and A

Test	Number of Items	Suggested Working Time (in minutes)
1 Reading	50	50
2 Mathematics Computation	40	24
3 Applied Mathematics	50	50
4 Language	55	55
5 Vocabulary	20	14
6 Language Mechanics	20	14
7 Spelling	20	10

Test 1 Reading

This test measures basic reading skills. The main concepts covered by this test are word meaning, critical thinking, and understanding basic information.

Test 2 Mathematics Computation

This test covers adding, subtracting, multiplying, and dividing. On this test, you must use these skills with whole numbers and decimals.

Test 3 Applied Mathematics

This test links mathematical ideas to real-world situations. Skills you do every day, such as budgeting, cooking, and doing your taxes, all require math. This test covers pre-algebra, algebra, and geometry, too.

Test 4 Language

This test requires you to analyze different types of writing, such as business letters, resumes, job reports, and essays. For each task, you have to show you understand good writing skills.

Test 5 Vocabulary

This test measures how well you can identify the meanings of words. You must also find words that mean the same or the opposite of some words. This test also measures whether you can find the meaning of a word with the help of other words in the same sentence or paragraph.

Test 6 Language Mechanics

This test measures how much you know about the elements that make a good sentence, such as capitalization and punctuation. You must also find the most important sentence, called the topic sentence, in a paragraph.

Test 7 Spelling

This test reinforces that you need to spell correctly, especially in the workplace. The spelling words on this test are words that many people misspell and words that are commonly used in adult writing.

Test-Taking Tips

1. Read the directions very carefully. Make sure you read them word for word. If you are not sure what the directions mean, ask the person giving the test to explain them to you.

2. Read each question carefully. Know what the question means and what you have to do.

3. Read all of the answers carefully, even if you think you know the answer.

4. Make sure that the passage supports your answer. Don't answer without checking the passage. Don't rely on outside knowledge alone.

5. Answer all of the questions.

6. Erase any extra marks before you finish.

7. Don't change an answer unless you are sure your first answer is wrong.

8. If you get nervous, stop for a while. Take a few breaths and relax.

How to Use *TABE Fundamentals*

Step-by-Step Instruction In Levels E, M, and D, each lesson starts with the step-by-step instruction of a skill. This instruction is followed by practice items. Check your work in the Answers and Explanations section in the back of the book. The Level A books only contain practice for each skill covered on the TABE. They do not include step-by-step instructions.

Reviews The lessons in Levels E, M, and D are grouped by TABE Objectives. At the end of each TABE Objective, there is a Review. Complete each Review before continuing to work.

Performance Assessment At the end of every book, there is a special section called Performance Assessment. This section will help you understand the actual TABE.

Answer Sheet At the front and back of each book, there is a practice bubble-in answer sheet. Fill in the answer sheet carefully. For each item, mark only one numbered space on the answer sheet. Mark the space beside the number that matches the item.

Strategies and Hints Pay careful attention to the TABE Strategies and Hints throughout the books. Strategies are test-taking tips. Hints give you extra information.

Setting Goals

Below is a form that will help you set your goals.

Section 1. Why do you want to do well on the TABE? Take some time now to set your short-term and long-term goals.

Section 2. Making a schedule is one way to set priorities. Deadlines will help you stay focused.

Section 3. Your goals may change over time. These changes are natural. Checking your progress on a regular basis helps you reach your goals.

1. Set Your Goals

What is your long-term goal for using this book?

_____

_____

Complete these lists to identify the smaller steps you need to take to reach your long-term goal.

Content area	What I Know	What I Want to Learn
Reading		
Language		
Math		
Other		

2. Make a Schedule

Set some deadlines for the goals you named in Section 1.

Goals	Begin Date	End Date

3. Celebrate Your Success

Note the progress you've made. If you made changes in your goals, record them here, too.

_____

_____

To the Instructor

About TABE

The seven Tests of Adult Basic Education in Reading, Mathematics Computation, Applied Mathematics, Language, Vocabulary, Language Mechanics, and Spelling are designed to meet the needs of adult learners in ABE programs. Written and designed to be relevant to adult learners' lives and interests, this material focuses on the problem-solving skills that are typical of adult needs. Because of the increasing importance of thinking skills in any curriculum, *TABE Fundamentals* focuses on critical thinking throughout the material presented for each TABE Objective.

Uses of the TABE

Instructional

From an instructional point of view, the TABE allows instructors to assess learners' entry level skills as they begin adult programs. The TABE also allows instructors to diagnose learners' strengths and weaknesses in order to determine appropriate areas on which to focus instruction. Finally, the TABE allows instructors and institutions to monitor learners' progress.

Administrative

The TABE allows institutions to assess classes in general and measure the effectiveness of instruction and whether learners are making progress.

Governmental

The TABE provides a means of assessing a school or program's effectiveness.

The National Reporting System (NRS) and the TABE

Adult education and literacy programs are federally funded and thus accountable to the federal government. The National Reporting System monitors adult education. Developed with the help of adult educators, the NRS sets the reporting requirements for adult education programs around the country. The information collected by the NRS is used to assess the effectiveness of adult education programs and make necessary improvements.

According to the NRS guidelines, states select the method of assessment appropriate for their needs. States can assess educational gain either through standardized tests or through performance-based assessment. Among the standardized tests typically used under NRS guidelines is the TABE, which meets the NRS standards both for administrative procedures and for scoring.

The three main methods used by the NRS to collect data follow:

1. **Direct program reporting**, which occurs from the moment of enrollment
2. **Local follow-up surveys**, which involve learners' employment or academic goals
3. **Data matching**, or sharing data among agencies serving the same clients, so that outcomes unique to each program can be identified

A key measure defined by the NRS is educational gain, which is an assessment of the improvements in learners' reading, writing, speaking, listening, and other skills during their instruction. Programs assess educational gain at every stage of instruction.

NRS Functioning Level	Grade Level TABE	TABE 9/10 Scale Scores
Beginning ABE Literacy	0–1.9	Reading........................367 and below Total Math....................313 and below Language......................389 and below
Beginning Basic Education	2–3.9	Reading........................368–460 Total Math....................314–441 Language......................390–490
Low Intermediate Basic Education	4–5.9	Reading........................461–517 Total Math....................442–505 Language......................491–523
High Intermediate Basic Education	6–8.9	Reading........................518–566 Total Math....................506–565 Language......................524–559
Low Adult Secondary Education	9–10.9	Reading........................567–595 Total Math....................566–594 Language......................560–585

Two of the major goals of the NRS are academic achievement and workplace readiness. Educational gain is a means to reach these goals. As learners move through the adult education curriculum, the progress they make should help them either obtain or keep employment or obtain a diploma, whether at the secondary school level or higher. The TABE is flexible enough to meet both the academic and workplace goals set forth by the NRS.

Using *TABE Fundamentals*

Adult Basic Education Placement

From the outset, the TABE allows effective placement of learners. You can use the *TABE Fundamentals* series to support instruction of those skills that need development.

High School Equivalency

Placement often involves predicting learners' success on the GED® Tests. Each level of *TABE Fundamentals* covers Reading, Language, Spelling, Vocabulary, Language Mechanics, and Applied and Computational Math to allow learners to focus their attention where it is needed.

Assessing Progress

Each TABE skill is covered in a lesson. These lessons are grouped by TABE Objectives. At the end of each TABE Objective, there is a Review. Use these Reviews to determine whether the learners need to review any of the skills before continuing to work.

At the end of the book, there is a special section called Performance Assessment. This section is similar to the TABE test. It has the same number and types of items. You can use the Performance Assessment as a timed pretest or post-test with your learners or as a more general review for the actual TABE.

Steck-Vaughn's *TABE Fundamentals* Program at a Glance

The chart on the following page provides a quick overview of the elements of Steck-Vaughn's *TABE Fundamentals* series. Use this chart to match the TABE objectives with the skill areas for each level. This chart will prove useful whenever you need to determine which objectives match the specific skill areas you need to cover.

Steck-Vaughn's *TABE* Fundamentals Program at a Glance

TABE OBJECTIVE	Level E		Level M		Level D		Level A
	Reading	Language	Reading	Language and Spelling	Reading	Language and Spelling	Reading, Language, and Spelling
Reading							
Interpret Graphic Information	◆		◆		◆		◆
Words in Context	◆		◆		◆		◆
Recall Information	◆		◆		◆		◆
Construct Meaning	◆		◆		◆		◆
Evaluate/Extend Meaning	◆		◆		◆		◆
Language and Mechanics							
Usage		◆		◆		◆	◆
Sentence Formation		◆		◆		◆	◆
Paragraph Development		◆		◆		◆	◆
Capitalization		◆		◆		◆	◆
Punctuation		◆		◆		◆	◆
Writing Conventions		◆		◆		◆	◆
Vocabulary							
Word Meaning		◆					
Multimeaning Words		◆					
Words in Context		◆					
Spelling							
Vowels		◆		◆		◆	◆
Consonants		◆		◆		◆	◆
Structural Unit		◆		◆		◆	◆

TABE OBJECTIVE	Level E	Level M		Level D		Level A
	Mathematics	Math Computation	Applied Math	Math Computation	Applied Math	Computational and Applied Math
Mathematics Computation						
Addition of Whole Numbers	◆	◆				
Subtraction of Whole Numbers	◆	◆				
Multiplication of Whole Numbers	◆			◆		
Division of Whole Numbers	◆	◆		◆		
Decimals	◆	◆		◆		◆
Fractions		◆		◆		◆
Integers				◆		◆
Percents				◆		◆
Order of Operation				◆		◆
Applied Mathematics						
Numbers and Number Operations	◆		◆		◆	◆
Computation in Context	◆		◆		◆	◆
Estimation	◆		◆		◆	◆
Measurement	◆		◆		◆	◆
Geometry and Spatial Sense	◆		◆		◆	◆
Data Analysis	◆		◆		◆	◆
Statistics and Probability	◆		◆		◆	◆
Patterns, Functions, Algebra	◆		◆		◆	◆
Problem Solving and Reasoning	◆		◆		◆	◆

Lesson 1 — Pronouns

A pronoun can take the place of a noun in a sentence. A personal pronoun takes the place of a specific person, place, or thing. It must function the same way as a noun in the sentence. If the noun is the subject of a sentence, the pronoun replacing it must be in subject form. The subject of a sentence names who or what the sentence is about. If the noun is the object of the sentence, the pronoun replacing it must be in object form. The object of a sentence tells who or what receives the action of the sentence.

Subject Pronouns		Object Pronouns	
Singular	Plural	Singular	Plural
I	we	me	us
you	you	you	you
he, she, it	they	him, her, it	them

Example Read the sentences. In the second sentence, choose the correct pronouns to replace the nouns *Jack* and *car*.

Jack owns a car. _____ bought _____ yesterday.
             (He/Him)   (them/it).

Did you select *He* and *it*? *Jack* is the subject of the sentence; he is only one person, and he is male. Therefore, you need the singular male subject pronoun *He* to replace the word *Jack*. *Car* is the object of the sentence. There is only one car, and it is not male or female, so you need the singular neuter object pronoun *it* to replace the word *car*.

Test Example

For Number 1, choose the word that best completes the sentence.

1   <u>Susan and Lamar</u> went on a hike. _____ climbed Snow Mountain.

    A   He   C   She

    B   They   D   Them

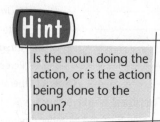

Hint

Is the noun doing the action, or is the action being done to the noun?

1 B *They* completes the sentence. Susan and Lamar are two people, so you need a plural pronoun. Susan and Lamar are completing the action, so you need a subject pronoun. Options A and C are singular pronouns. Option D takes the place of an object, not a subject, in a sentence.

Practice

For Numbers 1 through 6, choose the word that best completes the sentence.

1 Max is looking for a new job. _____ reads the want ads each day.

A It

B He

C Him

D They

2 Did you take your driving test? Did you think _____ was difficult?

F it

G we

H he

J she

3 The boys will be home soon. _____ will help clean the yard.

A He

B Us

C They

D Them

4 Keisha gave coats to Joe and Mark. The coats fit _____ perfectly.

F her

G him

H they

J them

5 Tom didn't go out with his friends. _____ didn't want to see the movie.

A He

B Him

C It

D Them

6 Yesterday, I called Jenny. I talked to _____ for about an hour.

F we

G us

H her

J she

Check your answers on page 95

Lesson 2 Verb Tense

A verb is a word or phrase that shows action. The tense of a verb tells when an action takes place. Did the action start and end in the past? Is it happening now? Will it happen in the future? On the TABE, you will be asked to use the correct tense of different verbs.

Example Read the sentence and write the verb that best completes the sentence. Should you use *need* (present tense), *needed* (past tense), or *will need* (future tense)?

Yesterday the boys _____ shovels to dig.

Did you write *needed*? The word *Yesterday* tells you the action took place in the past. The verb should be in the past tense. The chart below shows the past, present, and future tenses of some verbs.

Past	Present	Future
was, were	is, am, are	will, shall be
walked	walk	will walk, shall walk
hurried	hurry	will hurry, shall hurry

Most past tense verbs are formed by adding *–ed* to the end of the verbs. If the verb ends with a silent *e*, take off the *–e*; then, add the *–ed*. If the verb ends with a *–y* after a consonant, take off the *–y* and add *–ied*. For example, *carry - y = carr + ied (carried)*. Note that future tense verbs are usually formed by using the words *will* or *shall* before the present tense verb.

Test Example

For Number 1, choose the answer that is written correctly and shows the correct verb tense.

1 A The older men walk to work.

   B Yesterday I walk with Sam.

   C I walk with Jon next week.

   D Next week, I walk with Nick, too.

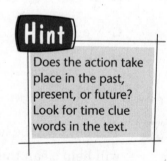

Hint

Does the action take place in the past, present, or future? Look for time clue words in the text.

1 A *Walk* is the present tense form of the verb. Nothing in the sentence points to the action taking place in the past or in the future. Option B contains the word *Yesterday* to show the action takes place in the past. Option C contains the words *next week* to show the action will take place in the future. Option D contains the words *Next week* to show the action will take place in the future.

For Numbers 1 and 2, choose the answer that is written correctly and shows the correct verb tense.

1 A I type that report a year ago.

  B Now I type much faster.

  C Tomorrow I type another report.

  D I will typed your report then, too.

2 F Brian was sick yesterday.

  G He was better now.

  H Sue is sick yesterday, too.

  J Sue was better tomorrow.

For Numbers 3 through 8, read the passage and look at the numbered, underlined parts. Choose the answer that is written correctly for each underlined part.

(3)   It is almost summer. Every year, we <u>plan</u> our vacation together. Right

(4)   now, I want to visit New York City, but later, I <u>listen</u> to everyone's ideas. Tonight,
       we each will put the name of the place we want to go on a sheet of paper.

(5)   Tomorrow, everyone <u>placed</u> his or her paper in a hat. Then my brother will
       pick one paper from the hat. The paper will name where we will go on vacation.

(6)   Last year, he <u>pick</u> my father's paper. Then our family visited the bay. We

(7)   sailed on the quiet waters. It <u>is</u> fun, but it was hot. Maybe next summer, we

(8)   <u>visit</u> some place cooler.

3 A will plan

  B planned

  C shall plan

  D Correct as it is

4 F had listened

  G listened

  H will listen

  J Correct as it is

5 A place

  B had placed

  C will place

  D Correct as it is

6 F picked

  G will pick

  H shall pick

  J Correct as it is

7 A was

  B shall be

  C will be

  D Correct as it is

8 F had visited

  G visited

  H will visit

  J Correct as it is

Check your answers on page 95

Lesson 3 | Subject/Verb Agreement

A subject must agree with its verb. Singular subjects agree with singular verbs, and plural subjects agree with plural verbs. The TABE will ask you to find verbs that agree with their subjects.

There are a few key things to remember about subject-verb agreement.

1 If the subject is singular, add *–s* or *–es* to most verbs.

    Ann reads.   Joe jumps.   It flies.

2 If the subject is plural, use the base form of most verbs.

    They read.   We jump.   Planes fly.

3 For the subjects *I* and *you*, use the base form of the verb.

    I read.   You jump.

4 Use the correct form of the verbs *be* and *have*.

Subject	Present Tense of *be*	Present Tense of *have*
I	am	have
He, She, It	is	has
You, We, They	are	have

5 Helping verbs convey time information and must agree with the subject.

    The store is closing.   The store will be closing.   The stores were closing.

Example **Read the sentence. Then choose the verb that best completes the sentence** *(teach/ teaches).*

    The chief of the local police _____ safety classes.

Chief is the singular subject. The singular verb is *teaches*. The subject and the verb must agree even when other words come between them.

Test Example

For Number 1, choose the answer that is written correctly and shows the correct subject/verb agreement.

1 **A** The girls plays golf together.   **C** My boss writes a report every day.

      B Elena buy the vegetables.   **D** The big dog are mine.

Practice

For Numbers 1 through 4, choose the word or phrase that best completes the sentence.

1 My friends _____ to start a Go Green program.

A want

B wants

C wanting

D is wanting

2 Each neighbor _____ something in the block garden.

F plant

G plants

H planting

J are planting

3 My friend _____ to pull weeds.

A offer

B offers

C offering

D are offering

4 The neighbors _____ Dave and Rita have a great plan.

F think

G thinks

H thinking

J is thinking

For Numbers 5 and 6, choose the answer that is written correctly and shows the correct subject/verb agreement.

5 A My neighbor have garden tools.

B He always share them with the group.

C Marco waters the garden.

D The new plants is starting to grow.

6 F Flowers gives the garden some color.

G Vegetable plants takes up most of the space.

H The friends plans to share the food.

J The neighbors work hard in the garden.

Check your answers on page 95

Adjectives describe nouns and pronouns and can be used to show comparisons. Adjectives improve writing by providing details and descriptions. To compare two things, use the comparative form of an adjective. To compare three or more things, use the superlative form.

Adjective	Comparative	Superlative
fast	faster	fastest
new	newer	newest
large	larger	largest
easy	easier	easiest
careful	more careful	most careful
important	more important	most important

Notice that most one-syllable words and words that end in –y usually end in –er in the comparative form and –est in the superlative form. Most adjectives with more than one syllable stay the same and use *more* in the comparative and *most* in the superlative. Other adjectives change completely.

Adjective	Comparative	Superlative
good	better	best
bad	worse	worst

Example   **Read the sentence. Circle the correct adjective.**

Shelby made a spicy chili, but Ricardo's chili was (spicier / more spicy / spiciest).

Did you circle *spicier*? Only two objects are being compared: Shelby's chili and Ricardo's chili. Use a comparative adjective. Since *spicy* ends in –y, drop the –y and replace with –ier. Ricardo's chili was spicier.

Test Example

For Number 1, choose the word that best completes the sentence.

1   Dayla is the _____ person I know.

   A   thoughtfuller

   B   most thoughtful

   C   thoughtfullest

   D   more thoughtful

1 B Since Dayla is being compared to every person the author knows, use the superlative form. Since *thoughtful* has more than one syllable, it will stay the same and the superlative word *most* will be added: *most thoughtful*. Options A and C are not the correct form. Option D would be used to compare only two things.

Practice

For Numbers 1 through 4, choose the word that best completes the sentence.

1 Tomas is _____ today than he was yesterday.

A happy

B happiest

C most happy

D happier

2 Troy had his _____ performance ever today.

F good

G better

H best

J gooder

3 Belinda rides her bike _____ than Monique.

A fast

B faster

C more fast

D fastest

4 The big dog is _____ than the small dog.

F friendly

G friendliest

H most friendly

J friendlier

For Numbers 5 and 6, choose the sentence that uses the correct adjective form.

5

A This essay is the most important assignment of the year.

B I have to do best on this essay than the last one.

C I think writing is more easy than studying.

D Shoi is the goodest student in class.

6

F My sister is looking for a more better car.

G She is studying car brochures to be a carefuller consumer.

H She is wiser about cars than I am.

J Tomorrow she will visit the most large car lot in town.

Check your answers on pages 95–96

For Numbers 1 through 4, choose the word or phrase that best completes the sentence.

1 Lynn _____ to lead next month's meeting.

   A want

   B wants

   C wanting

   D are wanting

2 The meeting next week _____ after the dinner hour.

   F start

   G started

   H starting

   J will start

3 I gave this month's notes to _____.

   A she

   B her

   C he

   D they

4 Mr. Patel ordered a _____ dinner than John ordered.

   F tastier

   G tasty

   H more tastiest

   J tastiest

For Numbers 5 through 8, choose the answer that is written correctly.

5 **A** Her wanted a new book.

   B Him offered to buy it.

   C The man gave the book to her.

   D Her read the book right away.

6 **F** Yesterday I walk to the library.

   G Last week, I walked on my usual path.

   H Ken will walk there with me yesterday.

   J Tomorrow, we walked a different path.

7 **A** The girls in the choir sings my favorite song.

   B Kate and Nina has solo parts in the concert.

   C Meg and Lee want bigger roles in the show.

   D The boys sits in the audience and listens.

8 **F** I have a new bike.

   G I wants a pretty bike.

   H I has two bikes.

   J Jake have a new bike, too.

For Numbers 9 through 13, read the passage and look at the numbered, underlined parts. Choose the answer that is written correctly for each underlined part.

(9)　　When my family moved from the city, <u>we</u> faced many challenges.
The first was how we would move from place to place. Before the

(10)　move, we rode buses everywhere. After the move, I <u>will discover</u>

(11)　that we needed a car. Now, my wife <u>want</u> to learn how
to drive. She misses going places on her own.

(12)　It will be my job to teach <u>she</u> how to drive.

(13)　We <u>thinks</u> about this chore all of the time.

9 **A** us
　　 B me
　　 C them
　　 D Correct as it is

10 **F** discover
　　 G discovered
　　 H discovering
　　 J Correct as it is

11 **A** wants
　　 B are wanting
　　 C were wanting
　　 D Correct as it is

12 **F** I
　　 G we
　　 H her
　　 J Correct as it is

13 **A** think
　　 B is thinking
　　 C was thinking
　　 D Correct as it is

For Numbers 14 and 15, choose the answer that best completes the sentence.

14 Amir chose a _____ drink than his sister did.
　　 F tall
　　 G more tall
　　 H taller
　　 J tallest

15 Chi never went near the _____ house on the block.
　　 A scariest
　　 B scarier
　　 C more scary
　　 D scary

Check your answers on page 96

Lesson 5 ▸ Sentence Recognition

A complete sentence must have a subject and a predicate. The subject tells who or what is doing something. The predicate, which always includes the verb of the sentence, gives the reader information about what the subject is doing.

Example **Read the sentence. Draw one line under the subject. Draw two lines under the predicate. Is the sentence complete?** _____

The new boss gave me a raise.

The new boss is the subject of the sentence. The subject is made up of one or more nouns or pronouns. Adjectives that describe the nouns or pronouns are also part of the subject.

Did you draw two lines under *gave me a raise*? The predicate is made up of one or more verbs. Words that modify or tell about the verbs are part of the predicate, too. Words needed to make the verb's meaning clear are also part of the predicate.

The sentence has a complete subject and predicate. It is a complete sentence.

Example **Read the sentence. Draw one line under the subject. Draw two lines under the predicate. Is the sentence complete?**

Did you wash the dishes?

Sometimes a sentence asks a question, which can make it harder to identify the subject and predicate. One easy way to check whether the question is a complete sentence is to turn it into a statement. *Did you wash the dishes?* might become *You did wash the dishes.* The word *You* is the subject of the sentence. The phrase *did wash the dishes* is the predicate of the sentence. This question is a complete sentence.

Test Example

For Number 1, choose the answer that is written correctly. Be sure the answer you choose is a complete sentence.

1 A   My youngest sister, Eva.

   B   Danced in a Broadway show.

   C   We stood and clapped for her.

   D   Threw flowers on the stage.

Hint

When looking for a complete sentence, ask *who* or *what* is doing something. Then, ask *what* is being done.

Practice

For Numbers 1 through 6, choose the answer that is written correctly. Be sure the answer you choose is a complete sentence.

1
A The ground shook.
B Plates and glasses.
C Fell from the shelf.
D The evening news.

2
F The pink and white tablecloth.
G A sunny, warm, spring day.
H I made egg and potato salad.
J The new park near our home.

3
A Driving down the road.
B I saw a new music store.
C Guitars, pianos, and drums.
D Pulled into the parking lot.

4
F Learned how to knit.
G Scarves, socks, and hats.
H Finished each knitting project.
J My sister bought more yarn.

5
A Could not hear you.
B The noisy crowd.
C Tried to hear.
D It didn't take long.

6
F To the city.
G Excited to be going.
H The show was wonderful.
J Wore beautiful costumes.

Check your answers on page 96

Good writers use both short and long sentences. Sometimes writers join together two or more short sentences to add variety or to keep from repeating words. The new, longer sentence must not change the meaning of the original sentences.

Example   **Read the sentences. Then write the sentences as one, new sentence.**

Steve worked today. Kim worked today.

_____

The best answer is *Steve and Kim worked today*. The verb is the same in both sentences. Using *and* between the subjects joins the two sentences into one sentence. This action does not change the meaning of either sentence.

Example   **Read the sentences. Then write the two sentences as one, new sentence.**

Don and Lori hiked today. Don and Lori swam today.

_____

The best answer is *Don and Lori hiked and swam today*. The subject is the same in both sentences. Using *and* between the verbs joins the two sentences into one sentence. The meaning of the original sentences stays the same.

Test Example

For Number 1, read the underlined sentences. Then choose the sentence that best combines those sentences into one.

1 Max knows Dan's family.
   Rick knows Dan's family.

   A   Max and Rick know Dan's family.

   B   Max knows Rick and Dan's family.

   C   Max, Rick, and Dan know his family.

   D   Max knows Dan's family, and Rick knows Dan's family.

TABE Strategy

Read test directions carefully. The word *best* is an important clue in some directions.

1   A   This option joins the sentences without changing the meaning of the original sentences. Options B and C cut extra words but change the meaning of the original sentences. Option D is not the best choice because it is too wordy.

For Numbers 1 through 5, read the underlined sentences. Then choose the sentence that best combines those sentences into one.

1 We had soup for lunch.
We had sandwiches for lunch.

A We had soup for lunch, and we had sandwiches for lunch.

B We had soup for lunch and sandwiches for lunch.

C We had soup, and we had sandwiches for lunch.

D We had soup and sandwiches for lunch.

2 I gave my son milk.
I gave my daughter juice.

F I gave my son and daughter milk and juice.

G I gave my son milk and my daughter juice.

H I gave my son and daughter juice.

J I gave milk and juice to my children.

3 I lost my cell phone.
Nina lost her cell phone.

A I lost my cell phone, and Nina lost it, too.

B Nina and I both lost our cell phones.

C I lost Nina and my cell phone.

D I lost my cell phone, and Nina lost her cell phone.

4 The nurse showed us how to bathe the baby.
The nurse showed us how to dress the baby.

F The nurse showed us how to bathe and dress the baby.

G The nurse showed us how to bathe the baby and also how to dress the baby.

H The nurse showed us how to bathe the baby and how to dress the baby.

J The nurse showed us how to bathe and dress.

5 The boys in the family like to play soccer.
The girls in the family like to play soccer, too.

A The boys in the family like to play soccer with the girls.

B The boys and girls in the family like to play soccer.

C The boys in the family and the girls in the family like to play soccer.

D The boys and the girls like to play soccer in the family.

Check your answers on page 96

Level E

Lesson 6 • 19

For Numbers 1 through 7, choose the answer that is written correctly. Be sure the answer you choose is a complete sentence.

1   A   Laura's long brown hair.
    B   Kate went to beauty school.
    C   Cutting the latest hairstyles.
    D   Her very first customer.

2   F   Joe voted in the last election.
    G   Supported the same candidate.
    H   The clear winner of the race.
    J   Held a big party after it ended.

3   A   A loud, strange sound.
    B   Took the car to the garage.
    C   The man fixed the problem.
    D   The quiet engine.

4   F   Neighbor's new dog.
    G   Barks all night.
    H   Wakes up everyone.
    J   Meg called the police.

5   A   Went to the library yesterday.
    B   Borrowed an interesting book.
    C   My dog chewed the cover.
    D   The wet, torn mess on the floor.

6   F   I am looking for a new apartment.
    G   Has at least three bedrooms and baths.
    H   Is close to a train station or bus stop.
    J   Has a swimming pool and small garden.

7   A   Many real life stories.
    B   I enjoy going to a movie.
    C   A very small theater.
    D   Plays first-run films.

For Numbers 8 through 10, read the passage. Then choose the sentence that best combines the underlined sentences into one.

(8)   I started taking art classes. <u>In the first class, I learned about color. In the first class, I also learned about space.</u> The teacher

(9)   had us work with soft chalks. <u>I pressed the chalks on the paper. I rubbed the chalks on the paper.</u> I was surprised by the different

(10)   color shades I made with these practices. <u>My son wants me to teach him now. My daughter wants me to teach her now, too.</u>

8 **F** In the first class, I learned about color; and I learned about space.

   G I learned about color, and I learned about space in the first class.

   H In the first class, I learned about color and space.

   J I learned about color; and also, I learned about space.

9 **A** I pressed and rubbed the chalks on the paper.

   B I pressed the chalks, and I rubbed them on paper.

   C I pressed the chalks, and I rubbed the chalks on the paper.

   D I pressed and I rubbed the chalks on the paper.

10 **F** My son wants and my daughter wants me to teach them now, too.

   G My son wants me to teach him, and my daughter wants me to teach her.

   H My son wants me to teach my daughter now, too.

   J My son and daughter want me to teach them now.

Check your answers on page 97

Lesson 7 Topic Sentences

A paragraph is a group of sentences. All of the sentences are about one subject. The topic sentence tells the main idea. You often find the topic sentence at the beginning of a paragraph.

Example **Read the passage. The topic sentence is underlined.**

> <u>When you are building a new home, weather can be your friend or foe.</u> It is easier to work outside when the weather is not too hot or too cold. A sunny day is perfect for putting on a new roof. Rain or snow can slow a job. Days of wet weather can delay the finish date for the whole house. Since builders can't control the weather, they must learn to deal with it.

The first sentence is the topic sentence. It tells the main idea of the paragraph. The other sentences show why weather can be good or bad for building.

Test Example

For Number 1, read the passage. Then choose the sentence that best fills the blank in the passage.

1 _____ At the end of the month, we often don't know where our money went. We may even run short of funds. If we write down each expense, we will have a better understanding of our buying habits. We can then use our records to plan a budget.

A   We would both like better paying jobs.

B   Keeping track of spending is a good habit.

C   Some money from my paycheck goes right into my savings account.

D   We always try to buy supplies when they are on sale.

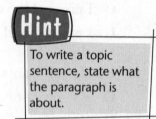

Hint

To write a topic sentence, state what the paragraph is about.

1 B This option states the main idea. The other sentences in the paragraph tell why keeping track of spending is a good habit. Options A, C, and D are about money, but they are not about tracking spending.

For Numbers 1 through 3, read the passage. Then choose the sentence that best fills the blank in the passage.

1 _____ Keep a list of things you need to buy and places you need to go. Group your places based on location. Combine errands that are near each other into one trip. Bring your lists with you. Avoid a second trip to buy or do something you forgot. Making fewer trips means using less gas.

   A Planning ahead can cut down on gas.

   B Buying in bulk means fewer shopping trips.

   C I never buy anything that isn't on a list.

   D Hang your lists in an easy-to-see place.

2 _____ How much does your audience already know about your subject? If they know very little, start with the basics. If they know a lot, give them new information. Also, think about the words and tone you use. Your words and tone should be different with children than with adults.

   G I have heard some great speeches this year.

   F When you give a speech, think about who is listening.

   H Do people know the sound of your voice?

   J Almost everyone has a favorite word or two.

3 _____ One neighbor is from China, another is from France. A family from Bermuda lives next door to us. We teach each other about our foods, music, and holidays. When we moved here from Canada, we were afraid we might not make friends. As it turns out, we moved to the perfect block.

   A It is colder in Canada in the winter than it is here.

   B The family in the blue house wears colorful clothes.

   C People from many different countries live on our block.

   D This winter, we learned how to celebrate the Chinese New Year.

Check your answers on page 97

A paragraph needs detail sentences. These sentences support the topic sentence. They may give examples, facts, or opinions about the topic.

Example Read the passage. The topic sentence is underlined.

> The brook brings many animals to my yard. Ducks and geese gather in or near the brook. The running water brings land animals, too. I often see deer sipping at the water's edge. Rabbits, foxes, and raccoons visit often. Even black bears walk into my yard looking for a drink.

What extra information is stated in the detail sentences about the main idea of the passage? _____

Did you notice that all of the detail sentences in the passage give more information about the kinds of animals that visit the speaker's yard, as well as the reasons the animals visit? All of the details support the topic sentence.

Test Example

For Number 1, choose the answer that best develops the topic sentence.

1 Walking is good for my body and mind.

A Even a short walk burns food. It gives me energy. Walking also helps me clear my mind. I forget about work and enjoy the world around me.

B Over the years, I have tried many activities. I used to swim every day. When my children were younger, we rode bikes. We played sports such as baseball. We even played tag.

C They are making a new walking path in the park. It will go around the pond. It will be three miles long. The new path should be ready by spring.

D I have a pair of sneakers for walking. They have a lot of padding in the soles. They feel great on my feet and keep me steady. I always wear them.

1 **A** The supporting sentences relate to walking and how it is good for the body and mind. While option B relates to physical exercise, it doesn't mention walking. The building of a new path in the park (Option C) doesn't relate to the topic sentence. Option D does not tell why walking is good for the body or mind.

Practice

For Numbers 1 through 4, choose the answer that best develops the topic sentence.

1 Everyone needs some quiet time in his or her life.

A I love walking near the ocean. The waves slapping the sand are noisy.

B Time passes very quickly. The busier we get, the faster time passes.

C Libraries are usually quiet. I live close to the library.

D Silence gives one a break from the outside world. The quiet gives one a chance to relax and gather one's thoughts.

2 The Statue of Liberty was like a big jigsaw puzzle.

F Workers broke the statue into pieces and shipped them to New York. In New York, people put the pieces back together again.

G One of my favorite things to do is put together puzzles. I always start with the frame and work inward.

H I have learned many things from books. I collect fun facts from each book I read.

J There are many landmarks in New York City. People visit the city every year to see them.

3 Walking in the woods is one of my favorite activities in the fall.

A The winter season is too cold for me.

B The changing colors of the leaves from green to red and orange are beautiful.

C Parks have many interesting plants and animals to see.

D Walking can be good exercise for anyone of any age.

4 It's fun to make your own pizza.

F Doing your own cooking is a wonderful way to make healthy food for yourself.

G After I spend a day cooking in the kitchen, I always have a lot of dishes to clean.

H You should use your favorite vegetables, such as peppers, mushrooms, and onions.

J We usually have pizza delivered to our apartment.

Check your answers on page 97

Lesson 9 | Sequence

A writer arranges detail sentences in an order that makes sense for readers. In time order, details are given in the order in which they happen. For example, seeing a hat comes before trying on a hat. Buying the hat comes after trying it on.

Example **Read the passage. Note the time order of the details.**

Our tour of the factory was interesting. First, we got on a bus. We rode to the rock pits. We watched workers mine large slabs of rock. Then we got back on the bus and rode to a big warehouse. Here, we watched workers cut the rock into smaller pieces. We learned a lot of information during the tour.

The topic sentence is first. The closing sentence is last. The detail sentences are between these two sentences. They are written in the order in which they happened.

Test Example

For Number 1, read the passage. Then choose the sentence that best fits the blank in the passage.

The storm caused us to change our plans for the day. When we saw the clouds, we quickly brought the games and decorations indoors. We set up the party for the second time. Then our guests started to arrive. _____ We played a few games before we ate. By the time we served the cake, it was raining.

Hint

Look for time order clues such as *first, last, before, after, next, then,* and *finally.*

1 **A** Then we ate the birthday cake.

  B We greeted our guests at the door.

  C We went outside to check the weather.

  D We set up the games outside.

1 **B** It makes sense the hosts would greet the guests after they arrive but before they play games. Option A belongs later in the passage, after the cake is served. Options C and D would come earlier in the passage, before the host brings everything indoors.

For Numbers 1 through 3, read the passage. Then choose the sentence that best fills the blank in the passage.

1 I decided to make something new for dinner. _____ I spent three hours preparing the food. My family ate the meal, but it did not taste good!

   A Finally I cleaned all the dishes.

   B My family left feeling hungry.

   C I looked through my cookbook for an idea.

   D The next day, I was not feeling well.

2 I first met Jonah in the train station. When we heard the whistle, we boarded the train together. We sat together in the last car. We spent hours talking. _____

   F I looked for an empty seat.

   G By the time we reached the city, we were friends.

   H I am planning to take the train into the city.

   J We waited for the train to start moving.

3 On Monday, I wrote a list of needed materials for building a dog house. In addition, I went to the store. The next day, I built the house. _____ Finally, on Friday, my dog moved into his new home.

   A Next I painted the house.

   B Then I double-checked my list.

   C First I chose a design.

   D Then I bought my supplies.

Check your answers on page 97

Lesson 10 Unrelated Sentences

A paragraph can have many sentences. However, all the sentences must relate to one main idea. Sometimes writers make mistakes and add sentences that don't belong in a paragraph. The TABE will ask you to find these kinds of sentences.

Example   **Read the passage. The underlined sentence does not belong in the passage. Why?**

My wife asked me to help paint the room. She showed me the paint color. <u>There are so many kinds of white paint.</u> Then she handed me a paint can and a brush! Minutes later, I was painting the wall green.

Example   **Read the passage. Find the sentence that does not belong. Draw a line under it.**

1. Last night, we went to the ball game. **2.** My little brother's favorite player made five hits. **3.** My little brother has this player's jersey. **4.** Each time the player got a hit, there were players on base. **5.** He helped six players score runs. **6.** He is the reason his team won the game.

Did you underline the third sentence? The paragraph is about a ball game. The sentence about the jersey does not belong. It does not tell more information about the game.

Test Example

For Number 1, read the passage. Then choose the sentence that does not belong in the passage.

1. Mike and Maggie went skating on the pond. **2.** There were many people on the ice, and everyone was having fun. **3.** Some people were sledding on the hill. **4.** Mike and Maggie skated around the people.

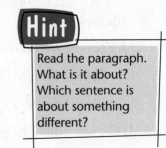

Hint

Read the paragraph. What is it about? Which sentence is about something different?

1 A   Sentence 1

   B   Sentence 2

   C   Sentence 3

   D   Sentence 4

1 **C**   Sentence 3 is about sledding, so it doesn't belong. The other sentences are about Mike and Maggie skating on the pond.

For Numbers 1 through 4, read the passage. Then choose the sentence that does not belong in the passage.

1 1. Bessie Coleman wanted to become a pilot. 2. No one in America would teach her how to fly a plane. 3. She worked for a newspaper. 4. She went to France to take flying lessons.

A Sentence 1

B Sentence 2

C Sentence 3

D Sentence 4

2 1. My aunt sent me some old family pictures. 2. They were pictures of my brothers and me when we were children. 3. Both of my brothers are farmers. 4. The pictures reminded me of the fun things we used to do.

F Sentence 1

G Sentence 2

H Sentence 3

J Sentence 4

3 1. A new store is opening in town. 2. It will sell racing bikes. 3. It is owned by a famous racer. 4. There is a bakery in town, too.

A Sentence 1

B Sentence 2

C Sentence 3

D Sentence 4

4 1. Thomas sorts his dirty clothes twice per week 2. Thomas mostly wears light colors in the summer. 3. He puts his light-colored clothes in a blue bin. 4. He puts his dark-colored clothes in a red bin.

F Sentence 1

G Sentence 2

H Sentence 3

J Sentence 4

Check your answers on page 97

For Numbers 1 through 4, read the passage. Then choose the sentence that best fills the blank in the passage.

1   Rock collecting is a fun and free hobby. Start by collecting rocks near your home. _____ Then tag each rock with its name.

   A   Fill a small pail with the rocks you find.

   B   Show your collection to a friend.

   C   I have a rock wall in my yard.

   D   Finally, find a safe place to keep your rocks.

2   _____ First, she learned how to do tricks. Then she learned how to make her own clown suits. Finally, she was ready to go to work.

   F   Next she learned how to make balloon animals.

   G   She learned how to fall without getting hurt.

   H   Her first job was with the circus.

   J   My cousin went to clown school.

3   Liz began playing the viola as an adult. Before long, Liz got tired of playing alone. _____ She started playing with a small, children's orchestra.

   A   Their music fit her skills.

   B   She wanted to join a group.

   C   The children wanted to help her learn.

   D   Liz never played music as a child.

4   Rob had to make many changes when he moved to Hawaii. _____ He couldn't find some of his favorite foods in the store. However, not all of the changes were bad. He liked that people did not always seem to be in a hurry.

   F   He missed riding the subway everywhere.

   G   He liked not needing a heavy winter coat.

   H   Before long, Hawaii felt like home.

   J   He loved spending time on the beach.

For Numbers 5 and 6, read the passage. Then choose the sentence that does not belong in the passage.

5 **1.** My friends all love to play card games. **2.** However, everyone seems to have his or her own rules. **3.** We play board games sometimes, too. **4.** Whenever we play, there is an argument over how a card is played or how a hand is scored.

  A Sentence 1

  B Sentence 2

  C Sentence 3

  D Sentence 4

6 **1.** It is easy to spot drivers from New Jersey at a gas station. **2.** They are the people at the gas pumps who don't know what to do. **3.** New Jersey is one of only two states that does not let people pump their own gas. **4.** New Jersey is also a great place to vacation.

  F Sentence 1

  G Sentence 2

  H Sentence 3

  J Sentence 4

For Numbers 7 and 8, read the passage. Then choose the sentence that best fills the blank in the passage.

7 _____ He invented the assembly line. At first, a worker did many jobs when building a car. Ford's line changed this practice. The cars moved from worker to worker. Each worker did a special job. Building cars this way was faster and cheaper.

  A Cars made it easier for people to travel.

  B Few families owned cars in Ford's time.

  C One of Henry Ford's cars was called the Model T.

  D Henry Ford changed the way many people worked.

8 _____ I like movies that make me laugh and movies that make me cry. I like learning new things from movies, too. There is nothing like seeing a show on the big screen.

  F Movie popcorn sometimes has too much salt.

  G They built a new movie house downtown.

  H One of my favorite things to do is go to a movie.

  J Clark Gable was a famous movie star.

Check your answers on pages 97–98

Lesson 11 First Words, Proper Nouns, Titles of Works

Capital letters are one of the tools writers use to make meaning clear for readers. They are used at the start of a sentence and for the names of people and places. Look at the chart. It shows several ways to use capital letters.

Kinds of Word	Examples
Names of specific people and places	Bob, Mrs. Smith, Dr. White, France, Statue of Liberty
Days, months, holidays	Monday, May, Thanksgiving
Titles of reading material and artwork	*War and Peace, The Washington Post, Starry Night*

Example **Read the sentences. Note the use of capital letters.**

Last year, Aunt Sue came to visit on New Year's Day.

The first word in the sentence begins with a capital letter. *Aunt Sue* is a name of a specific person. New Year's Day is the name of a holiday. All of these items start with capital letters.

We went to New York City to see a play on Broadway.

The first word in the sentence begins with a capital letter. *New York City* and *Broadway* are specific places. They each start with a capital letter.

Test Example

For Number 1, read the sentence and decide which part, if any, needs a capital letter. If no capital letter is missing, choose None.

1 When did	mr. Jones see	the Empire State Building?	None
A	B	C	D

1 B *Mr.* is a title. It is part of Mr. Jones's name.

For Numbers 1 through 3, read the sentence. Then choose the answer that does not show correct capitalization. If all the choices use correct capitalization, choose None.

1 My son Kevin | is a big fan | of the new york Yankees. | None
 A | B | C | D

2 My Aunt Diane's | birthday is | August 21. | None
 F | G | H | J

3 We had dinner | at Sammy's Steakhouse | on Sunday. | None
 A | B | C | D

For Numbers 4 through 6, read the passage and look at the numbered, underlined parts. Choose the answer that shows the correct capitalization for each underlined part.

(4)   Sam saw an ad in the newspaper for a copy of an old book, *My day of Fame,* for one
        dollar. Sam called Mrs. Ward and asked whether she still had the book. Mrs. Ward
(5)   told him to meet her at the corner of Pine street and Oak avenue. They met at noon on
(6)   Sunday. Sam bought the book and sent it to his cousin in Boston.

4 F *My Day of Fame*

 G *my Day of fame*

 H *My day of fame*

 J Correct as it is

5 A Pine Street and Oak Avenue. they

 B pine street and oak avenue. They

 C Pine Street and Oak Avenue. They

 D Correct as it is

6 F his Cousin in Boston.

 G His Cousin in Boston.

 H his cousin in boston.

 J Correct as it is

Check your answers on page 98

For Numbers 1 through 3, choose the answer that is written correctly and shows correct capitalization.

1 **A** We had a picnic on Labor day at Liberty Park.

  B Jamal saw the movie *One Step Closer* on Friday.

  C Mr. and mrs. Thomas went to the Grand canyon in July.

  D Pine Hill High school opens in early september.

2 **F** John Mullen is my great uncle.

  G Do you shop at Hay's market?

  H On Tuesday, mr. Rider went to the Morgan Museum.

  J Is Robert Packer the author of *A Love for all time*?

3 **A** Tom and Kim went to spain in the spring.

  B Jill sent Danny a postcard from Cape Cod.

  C The Main Street band gave a great show on Mother's day.

  D I saw a film about president Adams at the Grand Movie Hall.

For Numbers 4 and 5, read the passage and look at the numbered, underlined parts. Choose the answer that is written correctly for each underlined part.

New York is one of the most popular cities in the world. A visit to

(4) the city can start with a boat trip around the island of manhattan. The island is small, less than 23 square miles. However, it feels big because it is packed with tall buildings. The boat will cross three different

(5) rivers, the Hudson River, the East river, and the Harlem River. From the East River, visitors will get a close view of the UN building. From the Hudson River, they will see the Statue of Liberty and Ellis Island. They will also get a rare look at seven different bridges as they cross under each of them.

4 **F** the island of Manhattan.

  G The island of Manhattan.

  H the Island of manhattan.

  J Correct as it is

5 **A** east river,

  B east River,

  C East River,

  D Correct as it is

Check your answers on page 98

Lesson 12 End Marks

A sentence is not complete without an end mark. There are three end marks writers use to close sentences. A period (.) is used at the end of a telling sentence. A question mark (?) is used at the end of an asking sentence. An exclamation point (!) is used to show a strong feeling.

Example **Read the sentences. Then add the end marks needed.**

> 1. I saw Dr. Roberts today__ 2. Have you ever met her__ 3. She gave me some news__ 4. I am going to have a baby__

Did you add periods (.) after sentences 1 and 3? They are telling sentences. Did you add a question mark (?) at the end of sentence 2? It is an asking sentence. Did you put an exclamation point (!) at the end of sentence 4? It is a sentence that shows a strong feeling.

Period (.)	Use a period at the end of a telling sentence: *I went to the store.*
Question Mark (?)	Use a question mark at the end of an asking sentence: *Do you want to go?*
Exclamation Point (!)	Use an exclamation point to show strong feelings: *No! You cannot go!*

Test Example

For Number 1, decide which punctuation mark, if any, is needed in the sentence.

1 Bill will lend you his car

   A .

   B !

   C ?

   D Correct as it is

Hint

Read the sentence. Is it telling a fact? Is it showing a strong feeling? Is it asking a question?

1 A This telling sentence needs a period. It does not show strong emotion (Option B). It is not a question (Option C). The sentence is not correct as it is because it is missing an end mark (Option D).

For Numbers 1 through 8, decide which punctuation mark, if any, is needed in the sentence.

1 Our children met at the bus stop

   A   .

   B   !

   C   ?

   D   None

2 Yes! I won the money

   F   ?

   G   .

   H   !

   J   None

3 Where is the report

   A   .

   B   ?

   C   !

   D   None

4 There are three feet in one yard

   F   .

   G   !

   H   ?

   J   None

5 Have you ever seen the Grand Canyon

   A   !

   B   ?

   C   .

   D   None

6 I need some help with the soup

   F   .

   G   ?

   H   !

   J   None

7 Oh my goodness

   A   .

   B   !

   C   ?

   D   None

8 We finished our part of the puzzle

   F   .

   G   !

   H   ?

   J   None

Check your answers on page 98

Commas break sentences into units of meaning. They are used in many places. Look at each comma rule. Then read the examples.

Rule 1 **Use commas when you have a list of three or more things.**
Examples: *Kim, Pat, and I went out. We went to watch a movie, have lunch, and shop for clothes.*

Rule 2 **Use commas between dates, addresses, and place names.**
Examples: *My sister lives in Saratoga, New York. She moved there on Sunday, May 5, 1982.*

Rule 3 **Use a comma when you speak directly to someone.**
Examples: *Jack, do you want soup? Do you want soup, Jack? I need to know, Jack, whether you want soup.*

Rule 4 **Use a comma to set off an introductory word or a group of words that start a sentence and give extra information about the words that follow it.**
Examples: *Yes, we can go today. Unfortunately, Pam can't come with us. Before we go, I need to pack a bag.*

Rule 5 **Use a comma to set off a word or group of words that describe, or give more information about, the noun that comes before it.**
Example: *Mike, our team captain, asked me for help.*

Rule 6 **Use a comma between complete thoughts joined by a linking word.**
Example: *I will write the note, but I need more time to do it.*

Test Example

For Number 1, read the sentence and look at the underlined part.
Choose the answer that is written correctly for the underlined part.

1 She made salad, pasta and cake for us.

A made salad, pasta, and cake for

B made salad, pasta, and cake, for

C made salad, pasta, and, cake for

D Correct as it is

1 A The sentence needs commas after the words *salad* and *pasta*. Option B has an extra comma after *cake*. Option C has an extra comma after *and*. Option D is missing a comma after the word *pasta*.

For Numbers 1 through 4, read the sentence and look at the underlined part. Choose the answer that is written correctly for each underlined part.

1 Luis taught us how to sort, tag, and store the rugs.

A to sort, tag and store the

B to sort, tag, and store, the

C to sort, tag, and, store the

D Correct as it is

2 My problem, Laura is I don't have the time to do it.

F problem, Laura, is I

G problem Laura, is I

H problem Laura is I

J Correct as it is

3 I have a cold so I can't go.

A a cold, so, I

B a cold so, I

C a cold, so I

D Correct as it is

4 Kathy moved to Paris, France years ago.

F to Paris, France, years

G to Paris France years

H to, Paris, France, years

J Correct as it is

Check your answers on pages 98–99

For Numbers 1 through 4, decide which punctuation mark, if any, is needed to complete the sentence.

1   My brother, Dean, loves to go rock climbing

    A .

    B !

    C ?

    D None

2   He has no fear of high places

    F .

    G ?

    H !

    J None

3   Would I ever hang off the face of a mountain

    A .

    B ?

    C !

    D None

4   Not on your life

    F ?

    G .

    H !

    J None

For Numbers 5 and 6 choose the answer that is written correctly and shows correct punctuation.

5   **A** Have you ever been to Atlanta Georgia?

    B Have you ever been to Atlanta, Georgia?

    C Have you ever been to Atlanta, Georgia.

    D Have you ever been to Atlanta, Georgia!

6   **F** Mrs. White hired me to paint her house

    G Mrs. White hired me to paint her house!

    H Mrs. White hired me to paint her house?

    J Mrs. White hired me to paint her house.

For Numbers 7 through 10, read each sentence. Choose the answer that is written correctly for each underlined part.

7 My best <u>friend Beth is</u> a doctor.
   A friend, Beth is
   B friend Beth, is
   C friend, Beth, is
   D Correct as it is

8 She works in a hospital <u>in Morristown, New Jersey.</u>
   F in Morristown New Jersey.
   G in Morristown, New Jersey?
   H in Morristown New Jersey!
   J Correct as it is

9 She splits her time <u>among seeing patients, doing paperwork, and teaching</u> students.
   A among seeing patients, doing paperwork and teaching
   B among seeing patients, doing paperwork and, teaching
   C among, seeing patients, doing paperwork, and teaching
   D Correct as it is

10 It is hard <u>work but she loves it.</u>
   F work, but she loves it.
   G work, but she loves it?
   H work but she loves it!
   J Correct as it is

For Numbers 11 and 12, decide which punctuation mark, if any, is needed in the sentence.

11 This is the best gift I ever received!
   A ,
   B .
   C ?
   D None

12 Do you want to go to Space Park, or do you want to stay home
   F ,
   G ?
   H !
   J None

Check your answers on page 99

Lesson 14 Quotation Marks

Quotation marks are used to show words that are spoken. They tell exactly what has been said. Other punctuation marks are needed when using quotation marks, too. For instance, a comma follows the phrase that introduces the quotation. A period ends a quotation that also ends a sentence.

Example   My son said, "I would like to play catch."

If the quotation and the phrase are reversed, the comma goes inside the quotation marks and the period is at the end of the sentence.

Example   "I would like to play catch," my son said.

Whether the quotation starts the sentence or comes after a phrase, the first letter of the quotation is a capital letter.

Question marks and exclamation points may also end quotations. These punctuation marks belong inside the quotation marks.

Example   Benjamin asked, "Why don't we go outside and play catch?"

Test Example

For Number 1, choose the answer that is written correctly and shows correct punctuation.

1   A   You're late! my boss yelled.

    B   Come inside for supper," Mom said to Greta.

    C   The salesman said "This model gets the best gas mileage."

    D   Bill called Juanita and said, "There are some great sales at the mall."

1   D   This option correctly includes quotation marks around what Bill said and uses a comma to set off the phrase that introduces the quotation. Option A has no quotation marks around the speech. Option B lacks quotation marks at the beginning of the speech. Option C omits a comma after *said* to separate the phrase from the speech.

For Numbers 1 and 2, choose the answer that is written correctly and shows correct punctuation.

1
  A "Help me get up, I begged.

  B The general saluted and said, "Good work!"

  C "Roasted marshmallows are good" Jill told Frank.

  D Uncle Benny asked, "Why don't we take my car."

2
  F The teacher said, "take out your history books."

  G "All local schools are closed." reported the TV announcer.

  H Fishing is better below the dam," claimed my brother.

  J "My kitten climbed the tree, but she can't get down," Stacy cried.

For Numbers 3 through 6, decide which punctuation mark, if any, is needed in the sentence.

3 "Our subway stop is closed, my neighbor said.

  A "

  B .

  C ,

  D None

4 The vet asked "What happened to your dog?"

  F ,

  G "

  H ?

  J None

5 I screamed, "The house has been hit by lightning!"

  A "

  B .

  C ,

  D None

6 The guide announced, Follow me in a single file line, please."

  F ,

  G .

  H "

  J None

Check your answers on page 99

Lesson 15 | Apostrophes

Apostrophes have two uses. First, they are used to show possession. For singular nouns and for plural nouns that do not end in -s, add an apostrophe and an -s to show possession.

Example   **The bear's claws are very sharp.**

The children's coats were dirty.

With a plural noun that ends in an -s, add an apostrophe after the s.

Example   **All the girls' shoes were the same color.**

An apostrophe is also used to take the place of a missing letter or letters in a contraction. Contractions combine two words into one word by taking out one or more letters and replacing them with an apostrophe. Below is a table that shows some common contractions.

Contraction	Meaning
I'm	I am
he's, she's, it's	he is, she is, it is
you're, we're, they're	you are, we are, they are
isn't, wasn't, aren't, weren't	is not, was not, are not, were not

Contraction	Meaning
didn't	did not
doesn't	does not
won't	will not
can't	can not
don't	do not

Test Example

For Number 1, read the sentence and look at the underlined part. Choose the answer that shows correct punctuation for the underlined part.

1   In autumn, three of our maple <u>trees</u> leaves change color.

   A   tree's   C   tre's

   B   trees'   D   None

1 B   The plural of *tree* is *trees*. The plural possessive is formed by adding an apostrophe after the *s*.

For Numbers 1 and 2, read the sentence and look at the underlined part. Choose the answer that shows correct punctuation for each underlined part.

1 Please put <u>Ians books</u> on the desk.

   A Ians' books

   B Ians books'

   C Ian's books

   D None

2 His three <u>friends dogs</u> were strays.

   F friend's dogs

   G friends dogs'

   H friends' dogs

   J None

For Numbers 3 through 6, read the sentence and look at the underlined part. Then choose the answer that shows the correct contraction for the underlined part.

3 <u>It is</u> a good idea to work together on this project.

   A Its'

   B Its

   C It'is

   D It's

4 <u>Do not</u> forget to feed the dog.

   F Dont

   G Don't

   H Dont'

   J Do'nt

5 What do you think <u>she is</u> doing at the picnic?

   A she's

   B she'is

   C shi's

   D shes'

6 We <u>can not</u> reach the top floor from this stairway.

   F can'nt

   G can'not

   H can't

   J ca'nt

Check your answers on page 99

Understanding the parts of a letter can be useful in helping you apply for a job or write to a business or a school. The parts of a letter have special names.

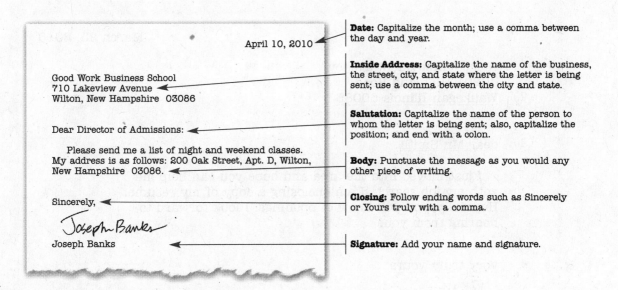

Date: Capitalize the month; use a comma between the day and year.

Inside Address: Capitalize the name of the business, the street, city, and state where the letter is being sent; use a comma between the city and state.

Salutation: Capitalize the name of the person to whom the letter is being sent; also, capitalize the position; and end with a colon.

Body: Punctuate the message as you would any other piece of writing.

Closing: Follow ending words such as Sincerely or Yours truly with a comma.

Signature: Add your name and signature.

Test Example

For Number 1, read the salutation from a letter. Choose the answer that is written correctly.

1 dear Mr. Peabody

   A Dear Mr. Peabody: C dear Mr. Peabody,

   B dear Mr. Peabody: D Correct as it is

1 A Option A starts with a capital letter and ends with a colon. In Options B and C, *dear* should be capitalized. Option C also requires a colon after *Peabody*.

For Numbers 1 through 4, read the letter and look at the numbered, underlined parts. Choose the answer that is written correctly for each underlined part.

March 23, 2010

(1) Acme employment agency
40201 Highland Road
(2) Waukegan Illinois 60085

(3) dear Mr. Smith

I just moved into the area and hope you can help me with my job search. I am enclosing a copy of my resume. Hopefully, you will know of openings. I look forward to hearing from you.

(4) very truly yours

Pao Vang

Pao Vang

1
A Acme employment Agency
B acme employment agency
C Acme Employment Agency
D Correct as it is

2
F Waukegan. Illinois
G Waukegan, Illinois
H waukegan, Illinois
J Correct as it is

3
A dear Mr. Smith:
B dear Mr. Smith,
C Dear Mr. Smith:
D Correct as it is

4
F Very truly yours,
G Very truly yours:
H very truly yours,
J Correct as it is

Check your answers on pages 99–100

For Numbers 1 and 2, decide which of the punctuation marks, if any, is needed in the sentence.

1 "Show me your driver's license" the policeman said.

   A "

   B .

   C ,

   D None

2 "Mike," Pete called, "get your baseball mitt"

   F ?

   G ,

   H .

   J None

For Numbers 3 and 4, choose the answer that is written correctly and shows the correct punctuation.

3 **A** "May I have my allowance early? I asked my mother.

   B "Why do you need money?" she responded.

   C I want to go to the new movie with Chris."

   D "Here's $10.00" she said.

4 **F** "Chris! I yelled to my friend through the phone.

   G "Not so loud" she answered.

   H I'm so happy!" I screamed.

   J "I bet we are going to the movies," Chris said.

For Numbers 5 and 6, read the sentence and look at the underlined part. Choose the answer that shows correct punctuation for the underlined part.

5 The <u>kittens fur</u> was matted and dirty after they were left in the woods for three days.

   A kittens' fur

   B kitten's fur

   C kittens fur'

   D Correct as it is

6 All the area farmers crops needed rain.

   F farmers crops'

   G farmers' crops

   H farmer's crops

   J Correct as it is

For Numbers 7 and 8, choose the answer that uses the apostrophe correctly in a contraction.

7 <u>I would</u> like to take the bus today.

   A Iw'ld

   B I'would

   C I'd

   D Id'

8 <u>He will</u> write a letter tomorrow.

   F He'll

   G He'wll

   H He'will

   J Hewill'

For Numbers 9 through 14, read the letter and look at the numbered, underlined parts. Choose the answer that is written correctly for each underlined part.

(9) September 15 2010

(10) Personnel department
(11) Fuller department store
602 Crawford Avenue
(12) Chicago Illinois 60606

(13) Dear director of personnel

I wanted to let you know how much I enjoyed shopping at your store last Thursday. The sales clerk Judy Jones was very helpful. She was able to help me find everything I needed.

(14) Sincerely,

Mrs. Franklin Carter-Smith

Mrs. Franklin Carter-Smith

9
A September 15, 2010
B September 15. 2010
C september 15, 2010
D Correct as it is

10
F personnel department
G Personnel department,
H Personnel Department
J Correct as it is

11
A fuller department store
B Fuller Department Store
C Fuller department store,
D Correct as it is

12
F Chicago Illinois, 60606
G Chicago, Illinois 60606
H chicago illinois 60606
J Correct as it is

13
A dear Director of Personnel
B Dear Director of Personnel,
C Dear Director of Personnel:
D Correct as it is

14
F sincerely
G Sincerely
H Sincerely:
J Correct as it is

Check your answers on page 100

Lesson 17 ▶ Synonyms

Synonyms are words with similar meanings. For example, a flower in a garden might be described as *pretty, beautiful, attractive, gorgeous,* or *lovely.*

Some words have similar meanings but are not synonyms. For instance, *puppy* and *dog* refer to similar animals, but there can be a difference in age. Puppies are dogs, but not all dogs are puppies. Thus, the two words are not synonyms.

Examples **We went to the local dealer to buy a <u>car</u>.**
We went to the local dealer to buy an <u>automobile</u>.

In the above examples, the words *car* and *automobile* are synonyms.

Test Example

For Number 1, read the sentence. Choose the word or phrase that means the same, or about the same, as the underlined word.

1 The woman was very <u>intelligent</u>.

　A tall　　　　　　C late

　B smart　　　　　　D hungry

1 **B**　*Intelligent* and *smart* are synonyms. The other answers may describe the woman, but they do not have the same meaning as *intelligent.*

For Numbers 1 through 6, read the sentence and look at the underlined part. Choose the word or phrase that means the same, or about the same, as the underlined word.

1 The children were all <u>giggling</u>.

A running

B unhappy

C fighting

D laughing

2 Put your books <u>under</u> your chair.

F below

G above

H over

J behind

3 The main road was <u>bumpy</u>.

A rough

B steep

C flat

D wide

4 The mountain was <u>big</u>.

F weak

G large

H sore

J strong

5 Dad will <u>clean</u> my pants.

A cover

B repair

C buy

D wash

6 The sign on the birdcage at the pet store read, "Please do not <u>tease</u> Captain."

F bother

G pet

H feed

J touch

Check your answers on page 100

Lesson 18 Appropriate Word

How do words work together in a sentence? Why is one word used instead of another? There are connections among words in a sentence that make meaning for readers. It is important to look for these connections to understand the meaning of a sentence.

Example   **Read the sentence. Determine which word fits best in the blank:** *bike, dog,* **or** *watch.*

Pasha took his pet _____ to the vet.

Did you pick *dog?* The words *pet* and *vet* in the sentence give you clues that an animal is probably the thing that fits in the blank. Using the other words in a sentence to create meaning is called using context clues. Good readers can use context clues to determine the meanings of unfamiliar words in a sentence.

Test Example

For Number 1, choose the word that best completes the sentence.

1   Chantal put the money from her paycheck in the _____.

A   library   C   office

B   school   D   bank

Hint

Ask yourself where people keep money.

1   **D**   A *bank* is the best place to put money. Options A, B, and C do not make sense in this context.

For Numbers 1 through 8, choose the word or phrase that best completes the sentence.

1 Let's stop at the furniture store. We need a new _____.

A car

B television

C couch

D phone

2 Gregor went to the doctor because he felt _____.

F sick

G happy

H full

J angry

3 The actors were dressed in costumes and ready to go on _____.

A the bus

B the plane

C stage

D time

4 I bought some apples at the _____.

F museum

G cleaners

H gas station

J grocery store

5 My garden is full of _____.

A books

B flowers

C cookies

D scissors

6 Melanie was _____, so she took a nap.

F tired

G angry

H scared

J happy

7 I rented a _____ at the video store.

A car

B flower

C house

D movie

8 Javier went to the beach to swim in the _____.

F ocean

G trees

H field

J boat

Check your answers on page 100

For Numbers 1 through 4, read the sentence and look at the underlined word. Choose the answer that means the same, or about the same, as each underlined word.

1 The <u>infant</u> cried loudly.

   A kitten

   B man

   C ring

   D baby

2 I <u>threw</u> the ball to my sister.

   F tossed

   G rolled

   H hit

   J took

3 Mom said my brother and I should not act <u>silly</u>.

   A tired

   B goofy

   C late

   D sad

4 The food they served was <u>awful</u>.

   F tasty

   G hot

   H terrible

   J hungry

For Numbers 5 through 8, choose the word or phrase that best completes the sentence.

5 There was no room in the parking lot. I had to park my car on the _____.

   A river

   B moon

   C street

   D fence

6 I put the eggs into the refrigerator to keep them _____.

   F scrambled

   G fried

   H cooked

   J cold

7 I needed to know what time it was, so I looked at my ____.

   A pillow

   B watch

   C glasses

   D table

8 When the waiter brought my salad, I asked for some _____.

   F dressing

   G books

   H socks

   J dirt

Check your answers on page 101

Lesson 19 Multimeaning Words

Figuring out the meaning of a word is sometimes like solving a puzzle. For example, some words are spelled the same but have different meanings. The best way to know what a word means is to read the sentence, or context, in which the word is found.

Examples The <u>lead</u> in Mary's pencil broke.
Jerry will <u>lead</u> the way down the path.

In the first example, *lead* is a noun that names part of a pencil. In the second example, *lead* is a verb that means "go first."

The fact that the word *lead* changes its meaning with its part of speech helps you figure out which meaning of the word is being used. The placement of a word in a sentence can also be a clue.

Examples Casey will <u>ship</u> out with the other Marines.
The <u>ship</u> is coming into the harbor.

In the first sentence, *Casey,* a noun, is the subject. *Ship* is part of the verb in the predicate. It tells the action. In the second sentence, the noun *ship* is the subject.

Test Example

For Number 1, choose the word that best completes <u>both</u> sentences.

1 My work load is very _____.
Turn off the _____ when you leave the room.

   A heavy   C light

   B television   D hard

> **1 C** *Light* is the only word that fits in both sentences. In the first sentence, *light* is an adjective. In the second sentence, *light* is a noun. The other options may fit one sentence but not both.

For Numbers 1 through 6, choose the word or phrase that best completes both sentences.

1 The _____ swam under the dock.
Pablo wanted to _____ on his vacation.

A fish

B turtle

C bicycle

D play ball

2 Rani needed a new battery for her _____.
Peder liked to _____ the news.

F read

G cell phone

H watch

J car

3 The _____ on the tree was smooth.
The dog's _____ was annoying.

A leaves

B owner

C bark

D tail

4 The students enjoyed the wrestling _____.
Here is a _____ to light the candle.

F lighter

G team

H program

J match

5 Emily wanted to go to the _____.
Do you know how to _____?

A sing

B dance

C movies

D mall

6 The metal _____ was bent.
My favorite season is the _____.

F winter

G rod

H spring

J summer

Check your answers on page 101

For Numbers 1 through 8, choose the word that best completes both sentences.

1 We all wanted to go to the school
_____.
The children went outside to
_____.

  A game

  B run

  C play

  D concert

2 The hockey arena had a new
_____ of ice.
The baby's crib had a clean _____
and blanket.

  F layer

  G linens

  H floor

  J sheet

3 I like to _____ my pony after a
long ride.
Hailey got a new comb and _____
for her birthday.

  A brush

  B pet

  C feed

  D dress

4 The roofer had to _____ a tall
ladder.
The path to the mountaintop was a long,
hard _____.

  F bring

  G climb

  H hike

  J carry

5 We _____ in Florida.
I always enjoy seeing a _____
show on stage.

  A stay

  B funny

  C live

  D great

6 Do you like to _____ scary books?
I have _____ many mysteries.

  F read

  G seen

  H carried

  J give

7 The young boy got a new _____.
It is relaxing to _____ a dog or
cat.

  A bike

  B toy

  C walk

  D pet

8 The workers had to _____ every
room.
Please buy more _____ at the
hardware store.

  F repair

  G paint

  H tools

  J supplies

Check your answers on page 101

Lesson 20 ▸ Words in Context

Sometimes, the context, or surrounding information, is the only way to figure out the meaning of a word. Unfamiliar words may be multi meaning words, homonyms, or new words. The other words, sentences, and information around unfamiliar words become the keys to unlocking the meaning of those unfamiliar words. These surrounding clues provide context.

You must use the context of the following sentences to decide meanings for the word *shoots*. It is only by reading the sentences that a meaning of "tender young plants" or "fires a gun" can be determined.

Examples There are new <u>shoots</u> sprouting in the garden.
Jeff <u>shoots</u> his new rifle at target practice every week.

You can also use context clues to figure out which word might be missing from a sentence.

Test Example

For Number 1, read the sentence. Choose the word that fits the context.

1 The _____ brought his hammer, level, and saws to the building site.

   A carpenter   C teacher

   B dancer   D bus driver

---

1 **A** Only a *carpenter* would use the tools that are listed. The other workers do not use these tools in their jobs.

For Numbers 1 through 6, read the passage. Then choose the word that best fills the blank in the passage.

Maria and Juanita only had one week for their (1)_____. They talked about what luggage to take and which (2)_____ to pack. Maria hoped the sun would shine each day so she could lie on the (3)_____. Juanita didn't care about the sun because she wanted to visit the history (4)_____. Both women knew they would have a good time visiting (5)_____ they had not seen in many months. They were (6)_____ to get ready for their wonderful trip.

1

A office
B vacation
C shopping
D work

2

F lunch
G tools
H pets
J clothes

3

A beach
B couch
C bed
D floor

4

F store
G book
H museum
J fair

5

A jobs
B offices
C relatives
D schools

6

F excited
G sad
H scared
J troubled

Check your answers on page 101

For Numbers 1 through 6, read the passage. Then choose the word that best fills the blank in the passage.

The students were excited about their trip to the (1)_____ museum, where they learned about different ways of travel. They first saw a (2)_____ with two wheels and long handle bars. Next, they saw old cars that were (3)_____ underground in one of the first subway tunnels. There were no boats in the museum, but the students saw a picture of small (4)_____ built to carry two people over the water. Finally, they were thrilled to be able to climb on a large, black (5) _____ that once had carried people in railroad cars across the country. it was a wonderful trip they would always (6)_____.

1
- **A** art
- **B** book
- **C** transportation
- **D** wildlife

2
- **F** bicycle
- **G** truck
- **H** horse
- **J** automobile

3
- **A** read
- **B** driven
- **C** fed
- **D** bought

4
- **F** trampoline
- **G** cruise ship
- **H** camel
- **J** canoe

5
- **A** horse
- **B** bicycle
- **C** truck
- **D** train

6
- **F** sleep
- **G** take
- **H** remember
- **J** drive

Check your answers on pages 101–102

Lesson 21 ▸ Short and Long Vowels

The alphabet is divided into two groups of letters: consonants and vowels. The vowels are *a, e, i, o,* and *u.* Vowels can make either a short sound or a long sound.

Vowels
Short Vowels • Vowels with a short sound often appear between two consonants, such as the *a* in *hat.* Long Vowels • Vowels with a long sound often need the help of a second vowel. • Sometimes the helping vowel appears directly after the long vowel. At other times, the helping vowel follows a consonant. • Long vowels can be formed by vowel pairs. Usually, the first vowel in a pair makes the long sound. The second vowel is usually silent. Study the following examples: the *ee* in *peel,* the *ie* in *pie,* the *ai* in *train,* the *i_e* in *bike,* and *o_e* in *home.* In *peel,* only one *e* is pronounced. In *pie,* the first vowel—the *i*—is the main sound. In *train,* the long *a* is the main sound. In *bike* and *home,* the final *e's* are silent. These *e's* give the first vowels in the words their long sounds.

Example Read the sentence aloud. Think about how the underlined vowels sound. They are examples of *short* vowels.

The m<u>e</u>n did n<u>o</u>t <u>o</u>bject to tipping the waiter.

Example Read the sentence aloud. Think about how the underlined vowels sound. They are examples of *long* vowels.

Shanna's b<u>i</u>ke is <u>e</u>asy to r<u>i</u>de.

Test Example

For Number 1, read the sentence and look at the underlined word. Choose the word that has the same vowel sound as the underlined word.

1 I love to <u>drive</u> my new car.

   A flip   C fir

   B time   D list

Practice

For Numbers 1 through 6, read each sentence and look at the underlined word. Choose the answer that has the same vowel sound as each underlined word.

1 There was no place for the settlers to live.

A tail

B tack

C rack

D slam

2 They had to build homes for shelter.

F mail

G take

H cape

J cat

3 They needed a place to sleep.

A feel

B bed

C fell

D met

4 They needed a place to eat.

F slept

G meals

H sent

J pets

5 They needed nails to make furniture.

A make

B mad

C tab

D can

6 They put mud and grass between the logs.

F grace

G fans

H hate

J fades

Check your answers on page 102

Lesson 22 R-controlled Vowels

Not all vowels have long or short sounds. Some words have pairs of letters that produce vowel sounds. Look at the word *bar.* This word does not have a short *a* sound even though the *a* appears between two consonants. Because the vowel is followed by an *r,* the strong sound of the *r* controls the sound of the vowel, producing an r-controlled vowel. In the case of *bar,* the *ar* sounds like "*are.*" Examples of r-controlled vowels include the following: *car, stir, corn,* and *hurry.*

Test Example

For Number 1, choose the word that best completes the sentence and shows an r-controlled vowel.

1   The cows are in the _____, waiting to be milked.

    A   pen   C   barn

    B   firm   D   shed

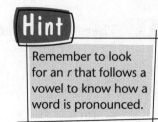

Hint

Remember to look for an *r* that follows a vowel to know how a word is pronounced.

1   **C**   *Barn* has an *r* that follows the *a.* The *a* does not have a short sound but makes a sound with the *r,* "ar." Option B has an r-controlled vowel, but the word does not make sense in the sentence. Options A and D do not have r-controlled vowels.

For Numbers 1 through 4, choose the word with an r-controlled vowel that best completes each sentence.

1 We were happy to be in the boat until we saw the _____.

A shack

B shark

C park

D space

2 The girl tried to smooth her _____ hair.

F curly

G blond

H brown

J party

3 The _____ planted his crops.

A man

B shopper

C farmer

D pilot

4 The _____ needed more gas.

F canoe

G trailer

H horse

J car

For Numbers 5 and 6, choose the word that best completes each sentence and shows an r-controlled vowel and correct spelling.

5 When do you start _____?

A werk

B work

C walk

D woke

6 It is important to have good _____.

F mannerz

G maners

H manners

J mans

Check your answers on page 102

For Numbers 1 through 8, read the sentence and look at the underlined word. Choose the answer that has the same vowel sound as each underlined word.

1 Feel free to visit soon.

A felt

B fled

C plea

D film

2 The stars shine brightly.

F shin

G piles

H shell

J pills

3 Do you play in a band?

A cage

B fan

C bed

D bird

4 Ben cut his finger.

F huge

G burn

H sun

J purple

5 Write your name on the line.

A nag

B mean

C fuel

D pail

6 It sure is hot!

F home

G crop

H adored

J more

7 Let's ride the huge roller coaster.

Roller Coaster

A cube

B cub

C hub

D home

8 All the rooms in the apartment have been painted white.

F lit

G when

H will

J file

For Numbers 9 through 12, choose the word that best completes the sentence and shows an r-controlled vowel.

9 The teacher _____ the test papers.

- **A** marked
- **B** parked
- **C** found
- **D** wrote

10 I rode a _____ while on vacation.

- **F** bicycle
- **G** farm
- **H** horse
- **J** train

11 Sari's coat is fuzzy and _____.

- **A** old
- **B** warm
- **C** red
- **D** hard

12 My parents _____ me to get a job.

- **F** told
- **G** begged
- **H** word
- **J** urged

For Numbers 13 through 16, choose the word that best completes the sentence and shows correct spelling.

13 George wanted to buy _____ for his girlfriend.

- **A** perlz
- **B** perls
- **C** pearlz
- **D** pearls

14 Fiona won an _____ for perfect attendance.

- **F** award
- **G** uhward
- **H** awerd
- **J** aware

15 Let's all go to the _____ in the park.

- **A** consert
- **B** concert
- **C** koncert
- **D** konsert

16 Paddle the canoe close to the _____.

- **F** shoar
- **G** shoor
- **H** shore
- **J** shoore

Check your answers on pages 102–103

Lesson 23 Variant Spellings
Silent Letters
Double Letters

The alphabet is divided into two groups: consonants and vowels. The vowels include *a, e, i, o,* and *u*. All the other letters are consonants. The letter *y* is a consonant that makes the sound of a vowel at times.

Just as the vowels can make more than one sound, some consonants also make more than one sound. The letters *c* and *g* are two letters that make more than one sound. The letter *c* can sound like an *s*, as in *center*, or like a *k*, as in *cake*. The letter *g* can sound like a *j*, as in *germ*, or like a *g*, as in *good*.

Examples There are many c̲ats in the c̲ity
The little g̲oats are g̲entle.

Some words have consonants that are not spoken. They are silent. The letters are needed, however, to spell the words correctly. In the example below, the *k*, the *w*, and the *gh* are silent.

Example Do you k̲now̲ your neig̲h̲bor?

Consonants are sometimes doubled. The second letter is not pronounced, but it is needed to spell the word correctly.

Example Please buy more ap̲p̲les.

Test Example

For Number 1, choose the word that best completes the sentence and shows correct spelling.

1 Bob has a car and a boat in his _____.

A garaje   C garoje

B garage   D garoge

1 B *Garage* is spelled correctly. Options A, C, and D are misspelled.

For Numbers 1 through 8, choose the word that best completes the sentence and shows correct spelling.

1 A family of cats lives in the _____.

   A alee

   B aly

   C aley

   D alley

2 When there is no moon, it's a dark _____.

   F night

   G nite

   H nihte

   J neight

3 Please _____ the boxes to the basement.

   A carre

   B karry

   C carry

   D karre

4 _____ carefully to the instructions.

   F Lissen

   G Listen

   H Lissin

   J Liesen

5 The boys like to tell scary _____ stories at their sleepovers.

   A gost

   B ghost

   C gose

   D goat

6 Kaylee bought two soft _____ for her bed.

   F pills

   G pilloughs

   H pillows

   J pilos

7 My favorite breakfast is scrambled _____.

   A egz

   B eegs

   C egs

   D eggs

8 The form had a space for my _____.

   F ag

   G age

   H eje

   J aje

Check your answers on page 103

For Numbers 1 through 10, choose the word that best completes the sentence and shows correct spelling.

1   Kevin had to sign a _____ for his new job.

   A leter

   B letter

   C leeter

   D letteer

2   Farah bought a new _____ phone.

   F sell

   G sel

   H cel

   J cell

3   The new teacher _____ three classes.

   A taught

   B taute

   C tught

   D tagt

4   Workers placed a new stop _____ at the corner.

   F siene

   G sign

   H cine

   J signe

5   The large _____ showed information about the new amusement park.

   A bilboard

   B bilbored

   C billboard

   D bellbored

6   After losing her job, Sarah had a lot of _____.

   F deht

   G dett

   H det

   J debt

7   I got only one item _____ on the test!

   A rong

   B wrong

   C rung

   D worong

8   The tour group visited an old _____.

   F cassel

   G kastle

   H kassle

   J castle

9   Write the _____ in the test book.

   A answers

   B ansers

   C annsers

   D anssewrs

10   The family enjoyed the _____ as they drove.

   F senery

   G cenery

   H scenery

   J senrey

For Numbers 11 through 18, choose the word that best completes each sentence and shows correct spelling.

11 The river ran through the _____.

 A valee

 B valley

 C valey

 D vallee

12 The baby's stuffed animal was green and _____.

 F fussee

 G fussey

 H fuzy

 J fuzzy

13 Wash your hands to kill the _____.

 A germs

 B jerms

 C germms

 D jurms

14 The poem has a catchy _____.

 F rhyme

 G rhime

 H rhym

 J ryme

15 _____ your hair before leaving for work.

 A Kome

 B Kombe

 C Comb

 D Come

16 I had three new phone _____.

 F messages

 G mesages

 H messajes

 J messagez

17 I _____ that you read the directions.

 A sugest

 B sugjest

 C suggist

 D suggest

18 We have to sign up for a _____ court if we want to play at noon.

 F tenis

 G teniss

 H tenniss

 J tennis

Check your answers on page 103

Lesson 24 Homonyms

Even though some words sound the same, they may be spelled differently and have different meanings. Words that are pronounced the same but are spelled differently and have different meanings are called *homonyms*. Below is a table of some common homonyms.

your—belongs to *you* you're—contraction for *you are*	its—belongs to *it* it's—contraction for *it is*
to—"I want to learn" or in that direction too—also two—the number 2	there—"there is" or in that place their—belongs to *them* they're—contraction for *they are*
son—male child sun—star; source of light	here—"here is" or in this place hear—ability to sense noise

When you hear a word, you can often tell its meaning by how it is used in a sentence.

Example   Stop <u>by</u> to see me anytime.
Jane went to the store to <u>buy</u> groceries.

Read the sentences above aloud. Note that the words *by* and *buy* sound the same even though they have different spellings and meanings. The words *by* and *buy* are homonyms.

The way a homonym is used in a sentence helps you know which spelling to use.

Test Example

For Number 1, choose the word that best completes the sentence and shows correct spelling.

1   You did the _____ thing.

   A   write   C   right

   B   rite   D   righte

1   **C**   The word *right* in this sentence means "correct." In Option A, *write* means "put words on paper," which does not fit the meaning of this sentence. In Option B, rite means "the action of a group or a church," which does not make sense in this sentence. Option D shows an incorrect spelling.

For Numbers 1 through 8, read the sentence. Then choose the homonym that best completes the sentence.

1 _____ running too fast.

A You're

B Your

C Youe

D Yoar

2 I'm trying _____ help you.

F two

G too

H to

J toe

3 He _____ how to tell the story.

A now

B nose

C news

D knows

4 The _____ is my favorite flower.

F rosy

G raise

H rows

J rose

5 Would you prefer a ham _____ turkey sandwich?

A oer

B orr

C or

D oar

6 I'd like you to meet my _____ and daughter.

F sone

G sun

H sune

J son

7 Speak louder so I can _____ you.

A heer

B heare

C hear

D here

8 We _____ an entire pizza.

F ait

G eight

H aight

J ate

Check your answers on pages 103–104

Similar Word Parts
Roots
Suffixes and Inflectional Endings (plural)

To improve spelling, it is often helpful to study the structure of a word. Words can have different parts. The main part of any word is known as the base, or root, of the word. Words can also have different endings. These endings are called suffixes. Some suffixes are -*ed* and -*ing*. To make a word plural (more than one), most words end with the suffix -*s* or -*es*.

Examples The <u>flower</u> is bright yellow.
The <u>flowers</u> are pretty.
Cal put a juicy, ripe <u>tomato</u> on his salad.
I planted <u>tomatoes</u> in my garden.

Some words have endings that sound similar but are spelled differently. The only sure way to learn the correct spellings is to memorize the words. However, for some words, there are clues to correct spelling. For instance, the sound "*shun*" at the end of a word, as in *mention* or *information*, is **never** spelled *s-h-u-n*. There are several possible ways to spell this sound, including -*tion*, -*sion*, -*cian*, and -*cean*.

Test Example

For Number 1, choose the word that best completes the sentence and shows correct spelling

1 Use _____ when crossing the busy street.

   A causion   C caushin

   B caushun   D caution

Hint

If you don't know how to spell a "shun" word, use -*tion*, which is the most common spelling of the sound.

1 D The most common spelling for the word part pronounced "shun" is used in *caution*. Options A, B, and C are spelled incorrectly.

For Numbers 1 through 3, choose the word that best completes the sentence and shows correct spelling.

1 There were many rotten _____on the ground.

   A potatoas   **C** potatose

   B potatoh   **D** potatoes

2 Several _____ ate the lettuce in our garden.

   F rabbits   **H** rabbites

   G rabbit   **J** rabbitt

3 After the long ride, Janine had _____ sickness.

   A mosion   **C** mossion

   B motion   **D** mocean

For Numbers 4 through 6, read the sentence. Then choose the word that has same root as the underlined word.

4 He carried the heavy <u>box</u>.

   F books   **H** bakes

   G boxes   **J** fix

5 Is that a good way to <u>act</u>?

   A axe   **C** art

   B aces   **D** acting

6 Do you know how to <u>fix</u> this?

   F fax   **H** fixing

   G fake   **J** mix

Check your answers on pages 104–105

For Numbers 1 and 2, read the sentence and look at the underlined word. Choose the word that shows the correct root of the underlined word.

1 Glen and Ellie paddled their <u>canoes</u> across the lake.

    A canues

    B canoez

    C canoe

    D canu

2 Please pick up a copy of those <u>magazines</u>.

    F mag

    G magazine

    H magazinees

    J magazs

For Numbers 3 and 4, read the sentence and look at the underlined word. Choose the answer that shows the correctly spelled plural of the underlined word.

3 We saw many animals at the <u>zoo</u>.

    A zoos

    B zooes

    C zoes

    D zooss

4 Mrs. Gray carefully set the <u>teacup</u> on the saucer.

    F teacupes

    G teascupps

    H teascup

    J teacups

For Numbers 5 through 8, read the sentence. Then choose the homonym that best completes the sentence.

5 Everyone must turn off his or her _____ phone in the fancy restaurant.

    A scell

    B cell

    C sell

    D sele

6 We have to _____ very quiet.

    F be

    G been

    H bee

    J bea

7 The wind _____ hard during the storm.

    A bloo

    B blew

    C blue

    D bluw

8 I'm sad that the dog had to _____.

    F dye

    G day

    H diy

    J die

For Numbers 9 through 18, choose the word that best completes the sentence and is spelled correctly.

9 You can get a map at the ____ booth.

A information

B informacian

C informacean

D informasion

10 Sue has _____ dollars to spend.

F ate

G eight

H eaght

J aghte

11 Where are the best ice _____ in the area?

A arens

B arenases

C arenas

D arenaes

12 The baseball team _____ the game.

F won

G owne

H wone

J one

13 The new _____ movie was exciting.

A aktion

B action

C axsion

D acshun

14 The furniture store put "Do Not Sit" signs on all the _____ .

F soffas

G soefas

H sofaes

J sofas

15 The first _____ of the class is tonight.

A session

B setion

C seshun

D secean

16 Will you please bring the box of _____ with you to the game?

F basesball

G baseballes

H baseballs

J basesballs

17 What _____ do you play for the team?

A posicean

B position

C posision

D posishun

18 Callie _____ her bike to school every day.

F rohde

G rode

H road

J rowed

Check your answers on page 104

The Language Performance Assessment models the real TABE in format and length. It will help you understand how to take the real test. Allow yourself 55 minutes to complete the assessment. Check your answers on pages 104-106.

Sample A

   A Last night, we paint the shirts.

   B We have fun, but we made a mess.

   C We spilling water everywhere.

   D Later, I will iron the shirts.

Sample B

   F I can never find a place to park

   G It is a problem in the summer.

   H Too many people drive to the beach

   J How do you find a parking place.

Sample C

Simon cleaned the hall.
Jeff cleaned the hall, too.

   A Simon and Jeff cleaned the hall.

   B Simon cleaned and Jeff cleaned the hall.

   C Simon cleaned Jeff and the hall.

   D Simon cleaned the hall, and Jeff cleaned the hall.

Sample D

Has Wendy come home <u>yet. We</u> need to get started.

   F yet, we

   G yet. we

   H yet? We

   J Correct as it is

For Numbers 1 through 4, choose the word or phrase that best completes the sentence.

1 The snowstorm this year is _____ than the snowstorm last year.

A worse

B bad

C worst

D badder

2 Next week, they _____ to a new safety program.

F went

G going

H will go

J have gone

3 The girls _____ with their fathers.

A cook

B cooks

C is cooking

D has cooked

4 I saw Maria and Alice, so I waved to _____.

F she

G her

H they

J them

For Numbers 5 and 6, choose the answer that is written correctly.

5 A Jana, the new cook.

B A bowl of apples.

C Jana cleaned and cut the apples.

D The prettiest apple pie ever!

6 F Joined the fire department.

G My brothers Roy and Lenny.

H They attended training.

J The longest fire truck.

For Numbers 7 through 10 read the sentences. Then choose the sentence that best combines those sentences into one.

7 Rose watched the football game.
Stan watched the football game.

A Rose and Stan watched the football game.

B Rose watched the football game with Stan.

C Rose watched Stan watch the football game.

D Rose watched and Stan watched the football game.

8 Jamal and Carmine fix cars.
Mary fixes cars, too.

F Jamal and Carmine fix cars, and Mary fixes cars, too.

G Jamal, Carmine, and Mary fix cars.

H Jamal fixes cars, and Carmine fixes cars; and Mary fixes cars, too.

J Jamal and Carmine fix Mary's car.

Go On ▶

9   I bought a hammer.
     I bought nails.
     I bought a saw.

    A I bought and I bought and I bought.

    B I bought a hammer, nails, and saw.

    C I bought a hammer and nails, and I bought a saw.

    D I bought a hammer, bought nails, and bought a saw.

10   Don hit the ball.
     Don ran to first base.

    F Don hit the ball, and Don ran to first base.

    G Don hit the ball and first base and ran.

    H Don hit and ran the ball to first base.

    J Don hit the ball and ran to first base.

For numbers 11 and 12, read the passage. Then choose the sentence that does <u>not</u> belong in the passage.

11 1. My daughter wants a pet snake.
     2. Some snake bites need treatment.
     3. She says it will be easy to take care of it.
     4. She will keep it in a glass tank.

    A Sentence 1

    B Sentence 2

    C Sentence 3

    D Sentence 4

12 1. I bought a new bed pillow.
     2. The pillow is made with feathers.
     3. Shopping is one of my favorite things to do.
     4. The feathers make my eyes and nose itch.

    F Sentence 1

    G Sentence 2

    H Sentence 3

    J Sentence 4

For Numbers 13 through 19, read the passage and look at the numbered, underlined parts. Choose the answer that is written correctly for each underlined part.

(13)   Have you ever been to <u>Washington, DC? We</u> went there

(14)   during <u>our spring break There</u> are so many museums there.

(15)   We chose to visit the <u>air and Space Museum.</u>

(16)   <u>It aren't the newest museum,</u> but it is one of our

(17)   favorites. My sons love the plane <u>in the lobby. Them</u> stood

(18)   in front of it, and I took several pictures of <u>them? I came</u>

(19)   home with a book called <u>*the history of flight*.</u>

13   **A** Washington, DC. We
      B Washington, DC? we
      C Washington, DC! We
      D Correct as it is

14   **F** our spring break. There
      G our Spring break, There
      H our Spring break! there
      J Correct as it is

15   **A** Air and Space museum.
      B Air, and Space Museum.
      C Air and Space Museum.
      D Correct as it is

16   **F** isn't the newest museum
      G weren't the newest museum
      H wasn't the newest museum
      J Correct as it is

17   **A** in the lobby. Him
      B in the lobby. They
      C in the lobby! Them
      D Correct as it is

18   **F** them. I came
      G them! I came
      H them, I came
      J Correct as it is

19   **A** *the History of flight*.
      B *the history of Flight*.
      C *The History of Flight*.
      D Correct as it is

(20) April 10 2011

Smith & Smith Lighting
16 Pine Street
(21) York, Pennsylvania 12345

(22) Dear Mr. smith:

(23) Last month, me placed an order for a very expensive
(24) fan a floor lamp and a table lamp. I received the lamps.
(25) The fan never arrived However, my credit card was charged
(26) for the complete order. I ask you Mr. Smith is this fair?
Please look into this matter quickly.

Sincerely,

David Ward

David Ward

20 **F** April, 10, 2011
    G April 10, 2011
    H april 10, 2011
    J Correct as it is

21 **A** York Pennsylvania 12345
    B York, Pennsylvania, 12345
    C York Pennsylvania, 12345
    D Correct as it is

22 **F** Dear mr. Smith:
    G Dear Mr. Smith:
    H Dear, Mr. Smith:
    J Correct as it is

23 **A** Last month, I placed an
    B Last month, us placed an
    C Last month, them placed an
    D Correct as it is

24
  F fan, a floor lamp, and, a table lamp.
  G fan, a floor lamp and a table lamp.
  H fan, a floor lamp, and a table lamp.
  J Correct as it is

25
  A arrived. However,
  B arrived, However,
  C arrived? However,
  D Correct as it is

26
  F I ask you, Mr. Smith is this, fair?
  G I ask you Mr. Smith, is this fair?
  H I ask you, Mr. Smith, is this fair?
  J Correct as it is

For Numbers 27 and 28, choose the answer that best develops the topic sentence.

27 My mother loved cooking with apples.
  A She also loved to sew. She sewed all of my sister's and my dresses.
  B Apples grow in parts of Washington. Washington is in the Northwest.
  C She made apple pie and apple cake. She would bake, boil, and fry the fruit.
  D In Florida, oranges are grown in many people's yards. They are used for juice and snacking.

28 Arturo is training for a 10-kilometer race.
  F The local paper ran a story about racing. It gave some great tips.
  G His sister Meg is a swimmer. She likes to spend time in the pool.
  H Good running shoes keep your feet safe. They don't have to cost much.
  J He runs every day. He is trying to build up to that distance.

For Numbers 29 through 34, decide which punctuation mark, if any, is needed in the sentence.

29 Susan do you know Jason?
  A ,
  B .
  C !
  D None

30 Never He will never do that!
  F ,
  G .
  H !
  J None

31 Is D'Wayne, Selma, or Pat going today
  A ,
  B .
  C ?
  D None

32 Did Dr. Garza talk to your group?
  F ,
  G .
  H !
  J None

Page 81

Go On ▶

33 Phil took a nonstop flight to Salt Lake City Utah.

A   ,

B   !

C   ?

D   None

34 The town voted against new lights and fences.

F   ,

G   !

H   ?

J   None

For Numbers 35 through 40, read the passage and look at the numbered, underlined parts. Choose the answer that is written correctly for each underlined part.

MEMO

Date: June 27, 2010

To: All Staff

From: Josh Baker, Manager

Subject: Annual Party

Please note that our annual party will not be held on
(35) June 3. Our last memo mistakenly cited this date.
(36) It is the wrong date. The party will be on June, 6.
We will begin at noon. Please meet at the picnic tables
(37) in walnut St. Park, and bring your family. We will cook
(38) ribs hamburgers and hot dogs on the grill. We will also
have games and prizes for the kids. There is street
parking, and there is a parking lot two blocks away on
(39) chestnut St.
(40) in the event of rain the party will be held one week
later on June 13th.

We hope to see everyone on June 6th.

35
A   our last Memo

B   Ours last Memo

C   They last Memo

D   Correct as it is

37
A   Walnut st. park

B   walnut st. park

C   Walnut St. Park

D   Correct as it is

36
F   on June 6.

G   on, June 6.

H   on June 6,

J   Correct as it is

38
F   ribs, hamburgers, and hot dogs, on.

G   ribs, hamburgers, and hot dogs on

H   ribs hamburgers, and hot dogs, on

J   Correct as it is

39 **A** Chestnut St.

    B chestnut st.

    C chestnut Street

    D Correct as it is

40 **F** in the Event of Rain

    G In the event of rain.

    H In the event of rain,

    J Correct as it is

For Numbers 41 and 42, read the passage. Then choose the sentence that best fills the blank in the passage.

41 My new place does not allow dogs. This news pleased me. _____ It will be great to live without the noise.

    A My old neighbor let her dog bark all night.

    B I watch or read the news every day.

    C Some dogs are trained to help people.

    D My friend is moving to a new place, too.

42 There are some strange laws on the books. _____ In Iowa, it is against the law to kiss for more than five minutes. In Maine, people may not spit from a second floor window. Every state has at least one odd law.

    F Strange things happen all around the world.

    G Lawmakers work together to pass fair laws.

    H The police are the ones who have to make sure the laws are followed.

    J In Kansas, there is a law that says you can't wear a bee in your hat.

For Numbers 43 through 45, read the passage. Then choose the sentence that best fills the blank in the passage.

43 Moving is never easy. Before you start packing, you need to sort through your things. _____ Then you have to pack the boxes. No matter how well you plan, something always ends up lost or broken.

    A Better yet, hire someone else to pack for you.

    B My husband told me it is time to move again.

    C It's better to toss some things out before moving them to a new place.

    D Wrap things that might break, and use a strong tape to seal the boxes shut.

44 Have you ever taken a dance class? The last class I took was open to men and women. The men in class said their wives made them sign up. _____ Some even asked the teacher to add a few classes to the course.

   F It was a class in line dancing.

   G She was happy to add classes.

   H The teacher was thrilled by the change in their outlooks.

   J However, after a few lessons, they were all having fun.

45 _____ They spent a few years in London, England. They lived in Italy twice. Their latest overseas job was in Singapore. Now they are back in the United States.

   A My neighbors have lived all over the world.

   B My neighbors are good volleyball players.

   C We went on vacation with my neighbors.

   D My neighbors loaned me a suitcase.

For Numbers 46 through 49, decide which punctuation mark, if any, is needed in the sentence.

46 "Mom! I can't find my shoes! Cassie yelled.

   F !

   G "

   H ,

   J None

47 "What is your name" the reporter asked.

   A !

   B ,

   C ?

   D None

48 The lawn needs mowing again, Joey," Dad said.

   F ,

   G "

   H ?

   J None

49 Heidi asked "Do we have any eggs left?"

   A ,

   B ?

   C "

   D None

For Numbers 50 and 51, read the sentence and look at the underlined part. Choose the answer that is written correctly for each underlined part.

50 The <u>mouses nest</u> was in the old barn.

   F mouse's nest

   G mice's nest

   H mouses' nest

   J Correct as it is

51 Ray <u>did not</u> get the oil changed yet.

   A did'not

   B didn't

   C di'dt

   D didnt

For Numbers 52 through 55, read the passage and look at each numbered, underlined part. Choose the answer that is written correctly and shows the correct capitalization and punctuation for each underlined part.

(52) <u>January 2, 2011</u>

Ace Auto Repair
(53) <u>1900 Main street</u>
(54) <u>Minneapolis Minnesota 55317</u>

(55) <u>Dear Manager,</u>

52 **F** January 2.2011

   G january 2, 2011

   H January 2 2011

   J Correct as it is

53 **A** 1900 main Street

   B 1900 Main Street

   C 1900 main street

   D Correct as it is

54 **F** Minneapolis, Minnesota 55317

   G Minneapolis: Minnesota 55317

   H Minneapolis. Minnesota 55317

   J Correct as it is

55 **A** dear manager,

   B dear manager:

   C Dear Manager:

   D Correct as it is

STOP ✳

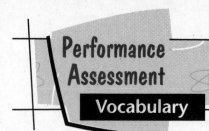
The Vocabulary Performance Assessment models to the real TABE in format and length. It will help you understand the real test. Allow yourself 14 minutes to complete the assessment. Check your answers on pages 106–107.

Sample A

<u>fresh</u> clothes

A dirty

B fruity

C clean

D ugly

For Numbers 1 and 2, read the sentences. Then choose the word that best completes both sentences.

1 The lawyer read Grandpa's _____ yesterday.
They _____ travel with us.

  A letter

  B should

  C can't

  D will

2 It's not polite to _____ at people.
The pencil has a sharp _____.

  F point

  G tip

  H spit

  J write

For Numbers 3 through 6, read the sentence and look at each underlined part. Choose the word that means the same, or about the same, as each underlined word.

3 The volunteers <u>improved</u> the park grounds.

  A enjoyed

  B repaired

  C destroyed

  D littered

4 I need to <u>park</u> the car.

  F tree

  G sit

  H playground

  J leave

5 The siding on the house was made of <u>wood</u>.

  A boards

  B forest

  C rotten

  D fur

6 Pam thought the birds were <u>noisy</u>.

  F quiet

  G loud

  H funny

  J pretty

Page 86

Go On ▶

For Numbers 7 through 10, choose the word or phrase that best completes the sentence and is spelled correctly.

7 The grass has not been cut for three weeks. It is very _____.

A short

B brown

C long

D green

8 I bought groceries at the _____.

F post office

G museum

H library

J market

9 Rafael read _____ at the library.

A muffins

B keys

C books

D trees

10 The nurse wanted a job. She applied at the _____.

F hospital

G restaurant

H zoo

J radio station

For Numbers 11 through 14, read the directions. Choose the correct answer.

11 Find the word that describes a baseball.

A round

B sharp

C pointed

D soft

12 Find the word that describes a person who is upset.

F shy

G happy

H sad

J joyful

13 Find the word that names what musicians do.

A instrument

B microphone

C sing

D guitar

14 Find the word that names a part of a fish.

F fin

G fur

H hook

J pole

For Numbers 15 through 20, choose the word that best completes the meaning of the sentence.

I washed my dog outside. To get her clean, I scrubbed her with ___(15)___. She was covered in bubbles. When I finished rinsing her off, she jumped out of the tub and ran around the ___(16)___. She rolled around on the ground. When she came back, she had ___(17)___ in her fur. Since she was dirty, I had to ___(18)___ her again!

15
A salt
B soap
C grass
D sticks

16
F yard
G subway
H restaurant
J hospital

17
A tables
B beds
C leaves
D gum

18
F wake
G hold
H feed
J wash

My sister went to the grocery store yesterday. She wanted to buy some ___(19)___ to make juice. When it was time to pay, she realized she'd left her ___(20)___ in the car. She had to run outside to get it.

19
A oranges
B cars
C art
D trees

20
F bee
G jacket
H gloves
J money

STOP ❋

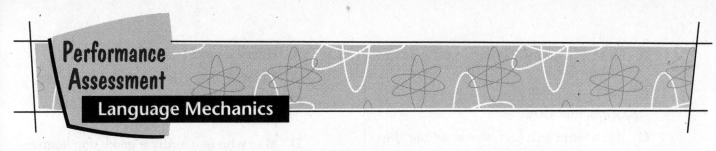

The Language Mechanics Assessment models the real TABE in format and length. It will help you understand how to take the real test. Allow yourself 14 minutes to complete the assessment. Check your answers on pages 107–108.

Sample A

A Have you ever jumped from a plane?

B My daughter has done this many times?

C She loves the way it feels to drift in the air?

D I don't think I could ever jump from a plane?

For Numbers 1 through 13, choose the answer that is written correctly and shows correct capitalization and punctuation.

1 **A** Do you know where the Chester Diner is located?

    B Kate's brother goes to Monmouth university.

    C Cars speed up and down Center street.

    D Mr. and Mrs. Garcia named the baby Alice marie.

2 **F** I wore a new dress to work today

    G I ate lunch with sam today.

    H Do you know Sam?

    J Have you ever met his brother.

3 **A** I read *a man and a Dog* last week.

    B My sister read *The Life and Times of a Nobody*.

    C We will trade books at Ray's ribs.

    D After that, we'll see the movie *My boy*.

4 **F** Have you ever gone skiing?

    G I tried to teach my children?

    H They kept falling in the snow?

    J They refused to ever try again?

5 **A** As you know, Lori, the dance is Friday.

    B Lori as you know the dance is Friday.

    C The dance is Friday as you know Lori.

    D Lori did you know the dance is Friday?

6 **F** we never bought a brand new car.

    G my husband says it is like throwing money away.

    H His dad also thinks it's a bad idea.

    J on the other hand, I long for the new car smell!

Page 89

Go On ▶

7
A Matt, Maya and Tim are on the same team.

B Sal is not on the team with Pat, Chris, and Guy.

C Each team will sort, stack, or, tag the materials.

D The work will take place in May June, and July.

8
F Does this bus stop at Market Street?

G It is located next to Tony's music.

H You need to take a bus to go to Center City High school.

J I'm going to Market street Plaza, not the high school.

9
A Would I say it if it wasn't true?

B Could I pay for her share

C I told Her I wasn't made of money.

D It wasn't fair to think I'd pay for her?

10
F Yes you can turn on the music.

G However keep the music low.

H No I never heard that band before.

J Thanks, but I can get it.

11
A Harry a good friend of ours is tall.

B His wife, Lucy, is tending the garden.

C Those flowers the purple ones are pretty.

D Mac who is usually a good dog keeps digging them up.

12
F The sun shone brightly, so I bought some sun block.

G I liked that but, it cost too much.

H This one blocks the sun, and, it has a nice smell.

J It was very sunny, yesterday but I don't think it is today.

13
A The wedding is June 15 2010.

B The church is in Mendham, Idaho.

C I was last there on March 11 2010.

D I stopped on my way to Dover Delaware.

For Numbers 14 through 16, choose the word that best completes the sentence and shows correct punctuation.

14 That _____ teacher left quickly.
    F classis   **H** classs'
    G class's   **J** classes'

15 The poor dog was lost, and no one could find _____ home.
    A its   **C** its'
    B itz   **D** it's

16 The kitten _____ come down.
    F would'ot   **H** wouldn't
    G w'ldnot   **J** w'uldn't

For Numbers 17 through 20, read the passage and look at the numbered, underlined parts. Choose the answer that is written correctly for each underlined part.

(17) January 14, 2011

Mrs. Emily Cisneros
421 Oak Avenue
(18) Dearborn Alabama 20101

(19) Dear Mrs. Cisneros

It was so much fun spending the holidays with you. I had a great time. I just got back home today and have to go to work tomorrow.
Thank you so much for everything.

(20) With love

Marcy

Marcy

17 A january 14, 2011,
    B January 14. 2011
    C january 14, 2011
    D Correct as it is

18 F Dearborn, Alabama 20101
    G Dearborn; Alabama 20101
    H dearborn, Alabama 20101
    J Correct as it is

19 A dear Mrs. Cisneros
    B Dear Mrs. Cisneros:
    C Dear Mrs. cisneros
    D Correct as it is

20 F with love
    G With Love:
    H With love,
    J Correct as it is

The Spelling Assessment models the real TABE in format and length. It will help you understand how to take the real test. Allow yourself 10 minutes to complete the assessment. Check your answers on page 108.

SAMPLE A

The baby was <u>sleepy</u>.

A rain

B pet

C meal

D time

For numbers 1 through 8, choose the word that is spelled correctly and best completes the sentence.

1 The store had a huge spring _____.

A sail

B sell

C sale

D seal

2 Grandma _____ the story aloud with a lot of feeling.

F raid

G reed

H red

J read

3 I called to say, "_____."

A High

B Hi

C Hih

D Hie

4 Please _____ the door.

F close

G clothes

H cloze

J class

5 The _____ was a good leader.

    A general

    B jeneral

    C jenral

    D genral

6 What is your favorite type of _____?

    F appel

    G apil

    H apple

    J aple

7 The boys practiced tying _____.

    A knots

    B notts

    C knotz

    D notz

8 The long _____ was dark and scary.

    F holloway

    G halway

    H holeway

    J hallway

For Numbers 9–12, read the phrases. Find the phrase that shows an underlined word that is not spelled correctly.

9   **A** car accident

    B black coffee

    C teacher's asistant

    D tiny footsteps

10   **F** relieve of duty

    G nite and day

    H hole in the ground

    J peace of mind

11   **A** beelieve in dreams

    B here to win

    C leaves in fall

    D pace back and forth

12   **F** aight girls playing

    G four fish swimming

    H whiff of vanilla

    J sense of sight

Go On ▶

For numbers 13 through 16, choose the letter of the word that is the correct spelling of the underlined word.

13 She made a <u>moshun</u> to be quiet.

   A motion

   B moshin

   C mowtion

   D mowshun

14 They liked to watch the news on <u>televizon</u> every night.

   F televishin

   G televishun

   H television

   J televizhun

15 I found a <u>rinkle</u> on my sleeve.

   A rrinkle

   B wrinkle

   C winkle

   D rwinkle

16 I poked my finger <u>throo</u> the hole in the cloth.

   F through

   G thoogh

   H though

   J tough

For Numbers 17 and 18, read the phrases. Find the phrase that shows an underlined word that is <u>not</u> spelled correctly.

17 **A** <u>terrible</u> noise

   B <u>shugar</u> cookie

   C <u>explore</u> the beach

   D <u>laughter</u> and tears

18 **F** new <u>adventures</u>

   G bad <u>decisiones</u>

   H monthly <u>allowances</u>

   J trained <u>musicians</u>

For Numbers 19 and 20, read the sentence. Choose the word that is spelled correctly and that best completes the sentence.

19 The three-year-old _____ his supper.

   A ate

   B aght

   C eight

   D aet

20 _____ mother called ten minutes ago.

   F Yoar

   G Yore

   H You're

   J Your

STOP ✳

Lesson 1 Practice (page 7)

1. B The pronoun *He* takes the place of *Max*. *Max* is the singular subject of the first sentence. Option A is incorrect because Max is a person, not a thing. Option C is incorrect because *Him* is an object pronoun. Option D is incorrect because it is a plural pronoun.

2. F The *driving test* is the singular object of the first sentence. *It* is a singular object pronoun. Options G, H, and J are all subject pronouns.

3. C *Boys* is the plural subject of the first sentence. The pronoun *they* is also subjective and plural. Option A is a singular pronoun. Options B and D are plural, object pronouns.

4. J *Joe and Mark* are the objects of the sentence and should be replaced by the plural, object pronoun *them*. *Her* and *him* (options F and G) are singular pronouns. Option H, *they*, is a subject pronoun.

5. A *Tom* is the singular subject of the first sentence. The pronoun must also be a singular subject: *He*. Options B and D are object pronouns. Option C describes a thing, not a person.

6. H *Jenny* is the singular object of the first sentence. The pronoun must also be a singular object pronoun: *her*. Options F and J are subject pronouns. Option G is plural.

Lesson 2 Practice (page 9)

1. B The word *Now* is a clue that the action happens in present time. The sentence needs the present tense verb *type*. Option A needs the past tense verb *typed*. Options C and D need the future tense form *will type*.

2. F *Was* is the past tense of *is*. The word *yesterday* is a clue showing that the action took place in the past. Option G uses a past tense verb to show an action happening now. Option H uses a present tense verb to show an action that happened in the past. Option J uses a past tense verb to show an action that will happen in the future.

3. D The action is happening now, so the sentence needs a present tense verb: *plan*. Options A and C are future tense verbs. Option B is a past tense verb.

4. H *Later* shows the action takes place in the future. The future tense form of *listen* is *will listen*. Options F and G are the past tense form. Option J is the present tense form.

5. C *Tomorrow* shows the action takes place in the future, so the correct verb form is *will place*. Option A is the present tense form. Options D and B are the past tense form.

6. F The action takes place in the past (*Last year*), so the past tense verb form, *picked*, is needed in the sentence. Options G and H are future tense forms. Option J is a present tense form.

7. A The sentence tells about something that happened last year. It needs a past tense verb: *was*. Options B and C are the future tense form. Option D is the present tense form.

8. H The sentence tells about something that might happen in the future. It needs the future tense form: *will visit*. Option J is a present tense verb, and options F and G are past tense verbs.

Lesson 3 Practice (page 11)

1. A *Friends* is plural, requiring the plural verb *want*. Options B and D are singular. Option C requires a helping verb.

2. G *Each neighbor* is a singular subject. *Plants* is a singular verb. Options F and J are plural verbs. Option H needs a helping verb.

3. B *Friend* is a singular subject that requires the singular verb *offers*. Options A and D are plural. Option C requires a helping verb.

4. F *Neighbors* is a plural subject, which requires the plural verb *think*. Options G and J are singular. Option H requires a helping verb.

5. C *Waters* is the correct singular verb for the subject *Marco*. Option A needs a singular verb and should read *has*. Option B needs a singular verb and should read *shares*. Option D needs a plural verb and should read *are*.

6. J *Work* is the correct plural verb for the plural subject *neighbors*. Option F needs a plural verb and should read *give*. Option G needs a plural verb and should read *take*. Option H needs a plural verb and should read *plan*.

Lesson 4 Practice (page 13)

1. D Use the comparative *happier* to compare today and yesterday. Option A is the adjective. Option B is the superlative. Option C does not make sense.

2. H Troy's performance today is being compared to every performance before it, so the superlative *best* is needed. Option F is an adjective. Option G is the comparative. Option J is not a real word.

3. B Use the comparative *faster* to compare Belinda and Monique. Option A is the adjective. Option C does not make sense. Option D is the superlative.

4. J Use the comparative *friendlier* to compare the two dogs. Option F is the adjective. Option G is the superlative. Option H does not make sense.

5. A *Most important* compares the essay to all other assignments. Option B incorrectly uses *best* to compare two things. Option C should use *easiest,* not *more easy. Goodest* is not a word (option D).

6. H This sentence correctly uses the comparative *wiser* to compare *she* and *I.* Option F incorrectly uses the word *more. Carefuller* is not a word (option G). Option J should use *largest,* not *most large.*

TABE Review: Usage (page 14–15)

1. B The singular verb *wants* matches the singular subject *Lynn.* Options A and D are plural verbs. Option C requires a helping verb. [Subject and Verb Agreement]

2. J The phrase *next week* tells about a future action, so the sentence needs a future tense verb: *will start.* Option F is a present tense verb. Option G is a past tense verb. Option H requires a helping verb. [Verb Tense]

3. B The pronoun *her* is the object of the action. The other options are subject pronouns. [Pronouns]

4. F The comparative form *tastier* correctly compares the two dinners. Option G is the adjective. Option H does not make sense. Option J is the superlative. [Adjectives]

5. C This option contains the pronoun *her* as the object of the action. The other options incorrectly use object pronouns as the subjects of the sentences. [Pronouns]

6. G Option G correctly uses a past tense verb; the phrase *Last week* provides a clue that the sentence needs a past tense verb. The other options have time clues such as *Yesterday* and *Tomorrow* that don't match the verb tenses in the sentences. [Verb Tense]

7. C *Meg and Lee* functions as a plural subject that requires the plural verb: *want.* The other options match plural subjects with singular verbs. [Subject and Verb Agreement]

8. F This option correctly combines the subject *I* with the present tense verb *have.* Option G should read *I want.* Option H should read *I have.* Option J should read *Jake has.* [Subject and Verb Agreement]

9. D *We* is the subject of the sentence. The other options are object pronouns. [Pronouns]

10. G *Discovered* agrees with *after the move* and *needed.* All show that the action takes place in the past. Option F is present tense. Option H requires a helping verb. Option J is incorrect because it uses *will* (used with future tense) and *needed* (past tense). [Verb Tense]

11. A The singular subject *wife* needs the singular verb *wants.* Options B, C, and D are plural verbs. [Verb Tense]

12. H The sentence needs the object form of a feminine pronoun: *her.* Options F, G, and J are subject pronouns. [Pronouns]

13. A The plural subject *We* requires the plural verb: *think.* The other options are singular verb forms. [Subject and Verb Agreement]

14. H *Taller* compares two glasses. Option F is the adjective. Option G incorrectly uses *more tall* instead of *taller.* Option J compares more than two things. [Adjectives]

15. A *Scariest* compares more than 2 houses. Option B is the comparative. Option C does not make sense. Option D is the adjective. [Adjectives]

Lesson 5 Practice (page 17)

1. A *The ground* is the subject. The predicate is *shook.* Option B and option D are subjects without predicates. Option C is a predicate without a subject.

2. H *I* is the subject. The predicate is *made egg and potato salad.* The other options are subjects without predicates.

3. B *I* is the subject. The predicate is *saw a new music store.* Options A and D are predicates without subjects. Option C is a subject without a predicate.

4. J *My sister* is the subject. The predicate is *bought more yarn.* Options F and H are predicates without subjects. Option G is a subject without a predicate.

5. D *It* is the subject and *didn't take long* is the predicate. Options A and C are predicates with no subjects. Option B is a subject without a predicate.

6. H *The show* is the subject and *was wonderful* is the predicate. Option F does not have a subject or predicate. Options G and H have predicates but no subjects.

Lesson 6 Practice (page 19)

1. D The subject and verb, *We had,* is found in both sentences. When this situation happens, use *and* to join the objects of the action (*soup* and *sandwiches*). The other options are wordier and repetitious.

2. G The subject and verb, *I gave,* is found in both sentences. When this situation happens, use *and* to join the objects of the action (*my son milk* and *my daughter juice*). The other options change the meaning of the original sentences.

3. B Both sentences have the same verb. To join the sentences, use *and* between the two subjects. Substitute *our* for *my* and *her* to show the plural subject. Options A and C change the meaning of the original sentences. Option D is too wordy and repeats several words.

4. F The subject and verb, *The nurse showed us,* are the same in both sentences. When this situation happens, use a single verb plus *and* to join the verbs (*bathe* and *dress*). Options G and H are too wordy and repeat words. Option J changes the meaning of the original sentences.

5. B The same verb is found in both sentences. Join the subjects with the word *and*; then remove the repeated words. Options A and D change the meanings of the original sentences. Option C is too wordy and repeats several words.

1. B *Kate* is the subject. The predicate is *went to beauty school*. Options A, C, and D are only subjects or predicates. [Sentence Recognition]

2. F *Joe* is the subject. The predicate is *voted in the last election*. Options G and J are predicates without subjects. Option H is a subject without a predicate. [Sentence Recognition]

3. C *Man* is the subject. The predicate is *fixed the problem*. Options A and D are subjects without predicates. Option B is a predicate without a subject. [Sentence Recognition]

4. J *Meg* is the subject. The predicate is *called the police*. Option F is a subject without a predicate. Options G and H are predicates without subjects. [Sentence Recognition]

5. C *My dog* is the subject. The predicate is *chewed the cover*. Option D is a subject without a predicate. Options A and B are predicates without subjects. [Sentence Recognition]

6. F *I* is the subject. The predicate is *am looking for a new apartment*. The other options are predicates without subjects. [Sentence Recognition]

7. B *I* is the subject. The predicate is *enjoy going to a movie*. Options A and C are subjects without predicates. Option D is a predicate without a subject. [Sentence Recognition]

8. H The sentence uses *and* between the two things learned about in class to join the sentences. The other options are wordy and repetitious. [Sentence Combining]

9. A The sentence uses *and* to join the verbs. The other options are wordy and repetitious. [Sentence Combining]

10. J The sentence uses *and* between the two subjects to join the sentences. Options F and G are wordy and repetitious. Option H changes the meaning of the original sentences. [Sentence Combining]

1. A The sentences in the paragraph are all about how to plan ahead to use your car less and save on gas. Options B, C, and D don't have anything to do with planning ahead to save gas.

2. F The sentences in the paragraph talk about basing your speech on who is listening. The other options are not related to audience.

3. C The sentences in the passage tell about neighbors and their home countries. Option A is not related to the subject. Options B and D are details that don't support the paragraph.

1. D These sentences tell why one needs quiet time. Option A talks only about the ocean. Option B tells about time passing. Option C talks about libraries.

2. F The detail sentences explain why the statue was like a puzzle. Options G, H, and J are not related to the the statue.

3. B This sentence provides details about walking in the woods. Options A, C, and D are not related to walking in the woods.

4. H Choosing your favorite vegetables is related to making pizza. The other options do not mention making your own pizza.

1. C It makes sense to use a cookbook before making the meal. The other options happen after the meal.

2. G It makes sense to reach the city at the end of the passage. Options F and H would have happened before meeting Jonah. Option J would have happened early in the trip.

3. A It makes sense to paint the house *after* building it and *before* the dog moves into it. The other options would be done before building the house.

1. C The passage is about Bessie Coleman becoming a pilot. Sentence 3 is not about Coleman becoming a pilot. It does not belong. The other sentences tell about Coleman becoming a pilot.

2. H The passage is about family pictures. Sentence 3 is about what the brothers do for a living. It does not belong. The other sentences tell about the pictures and how they make the speaker feel.

3. D The passage is about a new bike store. Options A, B, and C tell about the store. Option D is about a bakery. It does not give more information about the new store, so it does not belong.

4. G The passage is about sorting dirty clothes. Option G tells about wearing light-colored clothes. It does not belong.

1. A It makes sense to fill the pail with rocks when you start collecting them. Options B and D would come after tagging the rocks. Option C is not related. [Sequence]

2. J The topic sentence states the subject of the paragraph (*my cousin*) and what she did (*went to clown school*). All other sentences support this idea. Options F and G are details. Option H would come at the end of the passage. [Topic Sentence]

3. B The statement that Liz wanted to join a group makes sense after the statement that she was tired of playing alone. Options A and C belong later in the passage. Option D fits at the beginning of the passage. [Sequence]

4. F This sentence makes sense after the topic sentence—it describes something Rob misses due to the changes he had to make. Options G and J fit better after the sentence that says that not all the changes were bad. Option H belongs at the end of the passage. [Supporting Sentences]

5. C This option is the only sentence that is about board games. The other sentences describe playing card games with friends. [Unrelated Sentences]

6. J This is the only sentence that is about vacationing in New Jersey. The other options are about New Jersey drivers and pumping gas. [Unrelated Sentences]

7. D This topic sentence states the subject of the paragraph—Ford's assembly line changed the way people worked. The other options are about cars, not about a way of working. [Topic Sentences]

8. H This main idea ties together the other sentences about going to the movies. The other options tell about other aspects of movies. [Topic Sentences]

Lesson 11 Practice (page 33)

1. C This option needs capital letters for each part of the name *New York Yankees*.

2. J This sentence shows correct capitalization of the beginning of a sentence, a title, a name, and a month.

3. D There are no capitalization mistakes. The first word of the sentence starts with a capital letter. The sentence also uses a capital letter to begin the names of the restaurant and day.

4. F The important words in the title of the book are capitalized correctly in option F. The other options do not capitalize all the important words.

5. C This option uses capital letters at the beginning of the sentence and for the names of streets. In option A, *they* needs to be capitalized because it is the first word of the sentence. In options B and D, the full names of both streets need to be capitalized.

6. J The phrase is correct. *Boston* is capitalized because it is the name of a city. In option F, *Cousin* does not need to be capitalized. In option G, only *Boston* should be capitalized because it is the name of a city. In option H, *boston* should be capitalized because it is the name of a city.

TABE Review: Capitalization (page 34)

1. B The names Jamal, *One Step Closer*, and Friday are correctly capitalized. In option A, *day* needs to be capitalized because it is part of the name of a holiday. In option C, *mrs.* needs to be capitalized because it is part of a title of a person, and *canyon* needs to be capitalized because it is part of a proper noun. In option D, *school* needs to be capitalized because it is the name of the school, and *september* needs to be capitalized because it is the name of a month. [First Words, Proper Names, Titles of Works]

2. F The proper name John Mullen is correctly capitalized. In option G, *Market* should start with a capital letter. Option H needs a capital letter to start *Mr.* In option J, the first word and every important word in the title

should begin with a capital letter. [First Words, Proper Names, Titles of Works]

3. B The names *Jill, Danny*, and *Cape Cod* are correctly capitalized. Option A needs a capital letter to start *Spain,* the name of a place. Option C needs to start *Band,* which is part of a name, with a capital letter. The word *day* should also begin with a capital letter because it is the name of a holiday. Option D needs a capital *p* for *President* because the title is used as part of his name. [First Words, Proper Names, Titles of Works]

4. F *Manhattan* is the name of a place, so it is spelled with a capital letter. Option G is incorrect because *The* does not start with a capital letter. Options H and J are incorrect because *manhattan* should start with a capital letter because it is the name of a place. Option H is also incorrect because *Island* does not start with a capital letter. [First Words, Proper Names, Titles of Works]

5. C The names of places, such as rivers, begin with capital letters: the East River. Options A, B, and D are incorrect because both the words *East* and *River* should be capitalized. [First Words, Proper Names, Titles of Works]

Lesson 12 Practice (page 36)

1. A A telling sentence needs a period at the end.

2. H The sentence shows a strong feeling—excitement. It needs an exclamation point at the end.

3. B This sentence asks a question. It needs a question mark at the end.

4. F A telling sentence needs a period at the end.

5. B This sentence asks a question. It needs a question mark at the end.

6. F A telling sentence needs a period at the end.

7. B The sentence shows strong feeling—surprise. It needs an exclamation point at the end.

8. F A telling sentence needs a period at the end.

Lesson 13 Practice (page 38)

1. D A comma appears after each of the first two items in a series of three. Option A is missing a comma after *tag.* Option B has an extra comma after *store.* Option C has an extra comma after *and.*

2. F Commas set off a name when the speaker addresses a person. Option G is missing a comma before *Laura.* Option H is missing a comma before and after *Laura.* Option J is missing a comma after *Laura.*

3. C A comma appears before a linking word that joins two complete thoughts. Option A has an extra comma after *so.* Option B incorrectly places the comma after *so.* Option D is missing a comma before *so.*

4. J A comma appears between the names of places. Option F has an extra comma after *France*. Option G is missing a comma after *Paris*. Option H has extra commas before *Paris* and after *France*.

TABE Review: Punctuation (pages 39–40)

1. A The correct end mark for a telling sentence is a period. [End Marks]

2. F The correct end mark for a telling sentence is a period. [End Marks]

3. B The correct end mark for an asking sentence is a question mark. [End Marks]

4. H The correct end mark for a sentence that shows a strong feeling is an exclamation point. [End Marks]

5. B This asking sentence correctly uses a comma between the name of a city and state and ends with a question mark. Option A is missing a comma between the city and state. Option C uses a period instead of a question mark. Option D uses an exclamation point instead of a question mark. [Commas, End Marks]

6. J This option uses a period at the end of a telling sentence. Option F is missing an end mark. Options G and H use the wrong end marks. [End Marks]

7. C *Beth* gives more information about *friend* in the sentence. It must be set off by a comma before and after it. Option A is missing a comma after *Beth*. Option B is missing the comma before *Beth*. Option D is missing a comma before and after *Beth*. [Commas]

8. J This telling sentence correctly uses a comma between a city and state and ends with a period. Options F and H are missing a comma between the names of two places. Options G and H use the wrong end marks. [Commas, End Marks]

9. D This sentence correctly uses commas to separate items in a series. Option A is missing a comma after *paperwork*. Option B shows the comma after *and* instead of before *and*. Option C has an extra comma before *seeing*. [Commas]

10. F This telling sentence uses a comma before the word linking two complete thoughts. Option G uses the wrong end mark. Option H could possibly be read with strong feeling, but it is missing a comma. [Commas, End Marks]

11. D The sentence correctly ends with an exclamation point to show excitement. [End Marks]

12. G This asking sentence needs a question mark to end it. [End Marks]

Lesson 14 Practice (page 42)

1. B Option B uses quotation marks and punctuation correctly. Option A needs a quotation mark after the comma to close the quotation. Option C needs a comma *good* and before the ending quotation mark. Option D should have a question mark at the end of the quotation.

2. J Option J uses quotation marks correctly. The first letter in the quotation in option F (*take*) should be capitalized. Option G should have a comma, rather than a period, at the end of the quotation. Option H lacks quotation marks at the beginning of the quotation.

3. A The quoted material needs quotation marks after the comma to close the quotation. Options B and C are already in the sentence.

4. F A comma is needed after the phrase that introduces the quotation. Options G and H are already in the sentence.

5. D The sentence is correct as written and does not need any additional punctuation. Options A and C are already in the sentence. Option B is not needed because the sentence ends with an exclamation point rather than a period.

6. H Quotation marks are needed at the beginning of the quotation. Options F and G are already in the sentence.

Lesson 15 Practice (page 44)

1. C Ian is singular, so an apostrophe and an *s* are added to show possession of the books. Option A should have the apostrophe before the *s* in *Ians'*. Option B means that something belongs to the books, which is not the intended meaning.

2. H There is more than one friend, so the correct possessive form is *friends' dogs*. Option F refers to only one friend. Option G means that something belongs to the dogs, which is not the intended meaning.

3. D The *i* is dropped and replaced with an apostrophe in the contraction of *It is*. Options A and C are incorrect spellings of *it's*. Option B is the possessive form *its*, as in *Give the dog its dinner*.

4. G The *o* is dropped and replaced with an apostrophe in the contraction of *do not*. Options F, H, and J are incorrect spellings of the contraction *Don't*.

5. A The *i* is dropped and replaced with one apostrophe in the contraction of *she is*. Options B, C, and D are incorrect spellings of the contraction *she's*.

6. H The *n* and *o* are both dropped and replaced with one apostrophe in the contraction of *can not*. Options F, G, and J are incorrect spellings of the contraction *can't*.

Lesson 16 Practice (page 46)

1. C Each word in the name of a business needs to be capitalized. In options A, B, and D, the full name of the business needs to be capitalized.

2. G Both city and state names are capitalized. A comma separates the city from the state. Options F and J need a comma after *Waukegan*. In option H, *Waukegan* needs to be capitalized.

3. C The salutation begins with a capital letter and ends with a colon. In options A, B, and D, *dear* should be capitalized. In options B and D, a colon should follow *Smith*.

4. F The closing begins with a capital letter and ends with a comma. In options G and J, *yours* should be followed by a comma. In options H and J, *very* should be capitalized.

TABE Review: Writing Conventions (pages 47–48)

1. C A comma is needed between *license* and the quotation mark since the quotation comes before the explanatory phrase. Options A and B are already present in the sentence. [Quotation Marks]

2. H A period is needed at the end of this sentence. It is not a question, so it does not need a question mark (option F). Commas are already in place both before and after the explanatory phrase (option G). [Quotation Marks]

3. B Option B is correctly written. Option A is missing closing quotation marks after the question mark. Option C is missing the introductory quotation marks. Option D does not have a comma inside the closing quotation marks. [Quotation Marks]

4. J Option J is correct. Option F is missing the quotation marks after the exclamation point. Option G is missing the comma inside the closing quotation marks. Option H is missing the beginning quotation marks. [Quotation Marks]

5. A The word *they* is a clue that there is more than one kitten. The plural of *kitten* is *kittens*. To form the plural possessive, add an apostrophe after the *s*. Option B refers to only one kitten. Option C uses the apostrophe incorrectly. [Apostrophes]

6. G The word *all* is the clue that there is more than one farmer whose crops need rain. Thus an apostrophe is added after the *s*. Option F indicates that the crops possess something. Option H indicates there is only one farmer. Option J does not contain a possessive apostrophe. [Apostrophes]

7. C To form the contraction for *I would*, the letters *woul* are all dropped and replaced with an apostrophe. Options A, B, and D are incorrect contractions of *I would*. [Apostrophes]

8. F The contraction for *he will* is formed by dropping the *wi* in *will* and replacing it with an apostrophe. Options G, H, and J are incorrect contractions of *He will*. [Apostrophes]

9. A A comma is required to separate the day from the year. Option B has a period instead of a comma. Option C does not use a capital letter for the name of the month. [City/State, Letter Parts]

10. H The first letters of the name of a department should be capitalized. Option F does not capitalize the name. Option G has a capitalization error and an unnecessary comma after the name of the department. [City/State, Letter Parts]

11. B The first letter in each word in the name of the store should be capitalized. Option A does not capitalize the name. Option C does not capitalize the name correctly and has an unnecessary comma at the end of the line. [City/State, Letter Parts]

12. G Both the city and state need to be capitalized with a comma between them. There is no comma used between the name of the state and the zip code. Options F and H have comma errors. Option H also has capitalization errors. [City/State, Letter Parts]

13. C In a business letter, the salutation should begin with a capital letter and end with a colon. Option A does not capitalize the first word in the salutation and does not have a colon at the end. Option B has a comma at the end instead of a colon. [City/State, Letter Parts]

14. J The closing should be capitalized and end with a comma. Options F, G, and H have capitalization and/or punctuation errors. [City/State, Letter Parts]

Lesson 17 Practice (page 50)

1. D *Laughing* means the same as *giggling*. All other options have different meanings.

2. F *Below* and *under* are synonyms. All other options have different meanings.

3. A *Rough* and *bumpy* are synonyms. The other options have different meanings.

4. G *Big* and *large* are synonyms. Options F, H, and J do not mean the same as *big*.

5. D *Clean* and *wash* are synonyms. The other options have different meanings.

6. F *Tease* and *bother* are synonyms. The pet store may not want people to pet (option G), feed (option H), or touch (option J) the bird. However, the sign warns against teasing or bothering the bird.

Lesson 18 Practice (page 52)

1. C *Couch* fits best with the clue word *furniture*. Options A, B, and D would best be found at other kinds of stores.

2. F Because Gregor goes to see a doctor, he must be feeling *sick*. The other options would not require one to see a doctor.

3. C *Stage* matches the clue words *actors* and *costumes*.

4. J You can buy apples at a *grocery store*. The other options provide other goods and services.

5. B *Flowers* are what you would expect to find in a garden. The other options would not be found in a garden.

6. F *Tired* fits best with the clue word *nap*. The other options (angry, scared, and happy) would not make Melanie take a nap.

7. D *Movies* are rented at a video store. The other options (cars, flowers, and houses) are not rented at video stores.

8. F The beach is near the ocean, and you can swim in the ocean. You cannot swim in trees, a field, or a boat.

1. **D** *Infant* and *baby* are synonyms. The other options don't have the same meaning as *infant*. [Synonym]

2. **F** *Threw* and *tossed* are synonyms. The other options don't have the same meaning as *threw*. [Synonym]

3. **B** *Silly* and *goofy* are synonyms. The other options don't have the same meaning as *silly*. [Synonym]

4. **H** *Awful* and *terrible* are synonyms. The other options don't have the same meaning as *awful*. [Synonym]

5. **C** *Street* is the option that makes sense. You cannot park your car in a river, on the moon, or on a fence. [Appropriate Word]

6. **J** *Cold* is the option that makes the best sense with the context clue *refrigerator*. [Appropriate Word]

7. **B** *Watch* is the option that makes sense with the context clue *time*. [Appropriate Word]

8. **F** *Dressing* is the option that makes sense with the context clue *salad*. [Appropriate Word]

Lesson 19 Practice (page 55)

1. **A** *Fish* is the only word that fits both sentences. In the first sentence, *fish* is used as a noun. In the second sentence, *fish* is used as a verb. All other options fit only one sentence.

2. **H** *Watch* is the only word that fits both sentences. In the first sentence, *watch* is used as a noun. In the second sentence, *watch* is used as a verb. All other options do not fit in both sentences.

3. **C** *Bark* is the only word that fits both sentences. *Bark* is used as a noun in both sentences. All other options fit only one sentence.

4. **J** *Match* is the only word that fits both sentences. *Match* is used as a noun in both sentences. All other options fit only one sentence.

5. **B** *Dance* is the only word that fits both sentences. *Dance* is used as a noun in the first sentence and as a verb in the second sentence. All other options fit only one sentence.

6. **H** *Spring* is the only word that fits both sentences. *Spring* is used as a noun in both sentences. All other options fit only one sentence.

TABE Review: Multimeaning Words (page 56)

1. **C** *Play* is the only word that fits both sentences. *Play* is used as a noun in the first sentence. In the second sentence, *play* is a verb. All other options fit only one of the sentences. [Multimeaning Words]

2. **J** *Sheet* is the only word that fits both sentences. *Sheet* is used as a noun in both sentences. All other options fit only one of the sentences. [Multimeaning Words]

3. **A** *Brush* is the only word that fits both sentences. In the first sentence, *brush* is used as a verb. In the second sentence, *brush* is a noun. All other options fit only one of the sentences. [Multimeaning Words]

4. **G** *Climb* is the only word that fits both sentences. In the first sentence, *climb* is used as a verb. In the second sentence, *climb* is a noun. All other options fit only one of the sentences. [Multimeaning Words]

5. **C** *Live* is the only word that fits in both sentences. In the first sentence, *live* is a verb. In the second sentence, *live* is an adjective. All other options fit only one of the sentences. [Multimeaning Words]

6. **F** *Read* is the only word that fits in both sentences. In the first sentence, *read* is used as a verb in the present tense. In the second sentence, *read* is used as a verb in the past tense. All other options fit only one of the sentences. [Multimeaning Words]

7. **D** *Pet* is the only word that fits both sentences. In the first sentence, *pet* is used as a noun. In the second sentence, *pet* is used as a verb. All other options fit only one of the sentences. [Multimeaning Words]

8. **G** *Paint* is the only word that fits in both sentences. In the first sentence, *paint* is used as a verb. In the second sentence, *paint* is a noun. All other options fit only one of the sentences. [Multimeaning Words]

Lesson 20 Practice (page 58)

1. **B** *Vacation* is the only word that fits well with context clues such as *luggage*, *pack*, and *sun*. The other options are grammatically correct but don't make sense in the context of the paragraph.

2. **J** *Clothes* is the only word that fits well with context clues such as *luggage* and *pack*. The other options are grammatically correct but don't make sense in the context of the sentence.

3. **A** *Beach* is the only word that fits well with the context clues *sun* and *shine*. The other options are grammatically correct but don't make sense in the context of the sentence.

4. **H** *Museum* is the only word that fits well with context clues such as *visit* and *history*. The other options are grammatically correct but don't make sense in the context of the sentence.

5. **C** *Relatives* is the only word that fits well with context clues such as *visiting* and *not seen*. The other options are grammatically correct but don't make sense in the context of the sentence.

6. **F** *Excited* is the only word that fits well with the context clue *wonderful*. The other options are grammatically correct but don't make sense in the context of the sentence.

TABE Review: Words in Context (page 59)

1. **C** *Transportation* is the only option that makes sense with the context clue *travel*. The other options are grammatically correct but don't make sense in the context of the sentence. [Words in Context]

2. **F** *Bicycle* is the only option that makes sense with the context clues *two wheels* and *long handle bars*. The other options are grammatically correct but don't make sense in the context of the sentence. [Words in Context]

3. B *Driven* is the only option that makes sense with the context clue *old cars*. The other options are grammatically correct but don't make sense in the context of the sentence. [Words in Context]

4. J *Canoe* is the only option that makes sense with the context clues *small* and *over the water*. The other options are grammatically correct but don't make sense in the context of the sentence. [Words in Context]

5. D *Train* is the only option that makes sense with the context clues *large*, *black*, and *railroad*. The other options are grammatically correct but don't make sense in the context of the sentence. [Words in Context]

6. H Using the word *wonderful* as a clue, the only option that makes sense is *remember*. Although options F and J fit the grammar of the sentence, these choices do not make sense or support the meaning of the word *wonderful*. Option G take does not make sense in the sentence since the students already took the trip. [Words in Context]

Lesson 21 Practice (page 61)

1. A *Tail* is the only word with a long *a* sound as in *place*. All other options have a short *a* sound.

2. J *Cat* is the only option with a short *a* sound as in *had*. All other options have a long *a* sound.

3. A *Feel* is the only option with a long *e* sound as in *sleep*. All other options have a short *e* sound.

4. G *Meals* is the only option with a long *e* sound as in *eat*. All other options have the short *e* sound.

5. A *Make* is the only option with a long *a* sound as in *nails*. All other options have a short *a* sound.

6. G *Fans* is the only option with a short *a* sound as in *grass*. All other options have a long *a* sound.

Lesson 22 Practice (page 63)

1. B *Shark* has an r-controlled vowel and makes sense in the sentence. Options A and D do not have r-controlled vowels, and option C does not make sense in the sentence.

2. F *Curly* has an r-controlled vowel and makes sense in the sentence. Options G and H do not have r-controlled vowels, and option J does not make sense in the sentence.

3. C *Farmer* has an r-controlled vowel and makes sense in the sentence. Options A and D do not have r-controlled vowels, and option B does not make sense in the sentence.

4. J *Car* has an r-controlled vowel and makes sense in the sentence. Option F does not have an r-controlled vowel, and options G and H do not make sense in the sentence.

5. B *Work* is the only option that is spelled correctly and makes sense in the sentence. Options C and D do not have r-controlled vowels, and option A is misspelled.

6. H *Manners* is the only option that is spelled correctly and makes sense in the sentence. Options F, G, and J are misspelled.

TABE Review: Vowels (pages 64–65)

1. C *Feel* and *plea* have long *e* vowel sounds. Options A, B, and D have short vowel sounds. [Short and Long Vowels]

2. G *Shine* and *piles* have long *i* vowel sounds. Options F, H, and J have short vowel sounds. [Short and Long Vowels]

3. B *Band* and *fan* have short *a* vowel sounds. Option A has a long *a* vowel sound. Option C has a short *e* vowel sound, and option D has an r-controlled vowel. [Short and Long Vowels]

4. H *Cut* and *sun* have short *u* vowel sounds. Option F has a long *u* vowel sound, and options G and J have r-controlled vowels. [Short and Long Vowels]

5. D *Name* and *pail* have long *a* sounds. Option A has a short *a* vowel sound. Option B has a long *e* vowel sound, and option C has a long *u* vowel sound. [Short and Long Vowels]

6. G *Hot* and *crop* have short *o* vowel sounds. Option F has a long *o* vowel sound, and options H and J have r-controlled vowels. [Short and Long Vowels]

7. A *Huge* and *cube* have long *u* sounds. Options B and C have short *u* vowel sounds, and option D has a long *o* vowel sound. [Short and Long Vowels]

8. J *File* and *white* have long *i* vowel sounds. Options F and H have short *i* vowel sounds, and option G has a short *e* vowel sound. [Short and Long Vowels]

9. A *Marked* is the only word with an r-controlled vowel that makes sense in the sentence. Option B does not make sense in the sentence. Options C and D do not have r-controlled vowels. [R-controlled Vowels]

10. H *Horse* is the only word with an r-controlled vowel that makes sense in the sentence. Options F and J can be ridden but do not have r-controlled vowels. Option G does not make sense in the sentence. [R-controlled Vowels]

11. B *Warm* is the only word with an r-controlled vowel that makes sense in the sentence. Options A and C fit in the sentence but do not have r-controlled vowels. Option D does not make sense in the sentence. [R-controlled Vowels]

12. J *Urged* is the only word with an r-controlled vowel that makes sense in the sentence. Options F and G make sense in the sentence but do not have r-controlled vowels. Options H has an r-controlled vowel but does not fit in the sentence. [R-controlled Vowels]

13. D *Pearls* is the correct spelling. [R-controlled Vowels]

14. F *Award* is the only word that is both spelled correctly and makes sense in the sentence. [R-controlled Vowels]

15. B *Concert* is the correct spelling. [R-controlled Vowels]

16. H *Shore* is the correct spelling. [R-controlled Vowels]

1. D In this example of a double letter, the second *l* is silent. The *y* at the end of the word is also silent and gives the *e* in front of it a long *e* sound. Options A, B, and C are spelled incorrectly.

2. F *Night* has a silent *gh*. The *gh* combination usually gives the vowel in front of it a long sound. Options G, H, and J are spelled incorrectly.

3. C *Carry* is spelled correctly. Options A, B, and D are misspelled.

4. G *Listen* is spelled correctly. Options F, H, and J are misspelled.

5. B *Ghost* is spelled correctly. Options A, C, and D are either misspelled or do not fit the sentence.

6. H There is a double letter combination in *pillows* in which the second *l* is silent. The *w* at the end of the word is also silent and makes the *o* a long sound. Option F does not fit the sentence. Options G and J are spelled incorrectly.

7. D There is a double letter combination in *eggs* in which the second *g* is silent. The first *g* is a hard *g*. Options A, B, and C are spelled incorrectly.

8. G *Age* is an example of a soft *g*. Options F, H, and J are spelled incorrectly.

1. B *Letter* has double *t's*. Options A, C, and D are spelled incorrectly. [Double Letters]

2. J The *c* in *cell* is soft. In the double *ll* at the end of the word, the second *l* is silent. Option F does not fit the sentence. Options G and H are spelled incorrectly. [Double Letters]

3. A The *gh* in *taught* is silent. Options B, C, and D are spelled incorrectly. [Silent Letters]

4. G The *g* in *sign* is silent. Options F, H, and J are spelled incorrectly. [Silent Letters]

5. C In the double *ll* combination in *billboard,* the second *l* is silent. Options A, B, and D are spelled incorrectly. [Double Letters]

6. J The *b* in *debt* is silent. Options F, G, and H are spelled incorrectly. [Silent Letters]

7. B *Wrong* is spelled correctly. The letter *w* is silent. Options A and D are misspelled. Option C does not make sense in the sentence. [Silent Letters]

8. J *Castle* is spelled correctly. The letter *t* is silent. Options F, G, and H are misspelled. [Silent Letters]

9. A *Answers* is spelled correctly. The letter *w* is silent. Options B, C, and D are misspelled. [Silent Letters]

10. H The *c* in *scenery* is silent. Only the *s* is pronounced. Options F, G, and J are spelled incorrectly. [Silent Letters]

11. B In the double *ll* combination in *valley,* only the first *l* is pronounced. The second *l* is silent. Options A, C, and D are spelled incorrectly. [Double Letters]

12. J In the double *zz* combination in *fuzzy,* only the first *z* is pronounced. The second *z* is silent. Options F, G, and H are spelled incorrectly. [Double Letters]

13. A The *g* in *germs* is soft. Options B, C, and D are spelled incorrectly. [Variant Spellings]

14. F The *h* in *rhyme* is silent. Options G, H, and J are spelled incorrectly. [Silent Letters]

15. C The *c* in *comb* is hard. The *b* is silent. Options A, B, and D are spelled incorrectly. [Variant Spellings]

16. F *Messages* is spelled correctly. Options G, H, and J are misspelled. [Double Letters]

17. D *Suggest* is spelled correctly. Options A, B, and C are misspelled. [Double Letters]

18. J In the *nn* double letter combination in *tennis,* the second *n* is silent. Options F, G, and H are spelled incorrectly. [Double Letters]

1. A *You're* is a contraction for *you are*. *Your* is a homonym that means "belonging to you." Options C and D are misspelled.

2. H *To* is the correct answer. *Two* is a homonym for the number 2, and *too* is a homonym that means "also." Option J does not make sense in the sentence.

3. D *Knows* means "having information or understanding." *Nose* is "a part of the face." The two words sound the same but have different meanings. Options A and C do not make sense.

4. J *Rose* is the correct answer. Option H (*rows*) sounds the same as *rose*, but it does not make sense in the sentence. Options F and G do not make sense in the sentence.

5. C The homonym *or* makes sense in the sentence. Options A and B are misspelled, and the homonym *oar* (option D) does not make sense in the sentence.

6. J The homonym *son* is the correct answer. The homonym *sun* does not make sense in the sentence, and options F and H are misspelled.

7. C The homonym *hear* is the correct answer. The homonym *here* does not make sense in the sentence. Options A and B are misspelled.

8. J The homonym *ate* is the correct answer. The homonym *eight* does not make sense in the sentence. Options F and H are misspelled.

1. D The plural of *potato* is made by adding the suffix *-es*. Options A, B, and C are spelled incorrectly.

2. F The plural noun *rabbits* fits the context clue *several*. Option G is singular. The other options are not spelled correctly.

3. B The correct answer uses the most common spelling of the "shun" sound, which is -*tion*. Options A, C, and D are spelled incorrectly.

4. G *Boxes* has the same root as *box*. Options F, H, and J have different roots.

5. D *Acting* has the same root as *act*. Options A, B, and C have different roots.

6. H *Fixing* has the same root as *fix*. Options F, G, and J have different roots.

TABE Review: Structural Unit (pages 74–75)

1. C The root word of *canoes* is the singular form, *canoe*. Options A, B, and D are spelled incorrectly. [Roots]

2. G The root word of *magazines* is the singular form, *magazine*. Options F, H, and J are spelled incorrectly. [Roots]

3. A The plural of *zoo* is created by adding an -*s*. Options B, C, and D are spelled incorrectly. [Plurals]

4. J The plural of *teacup* is made by adding an -*s*. Options F, G, and H are spelled incorrectly. [Plurals]

5. B *Cell* is the correct answer. The homonym *sell* does not make sense in the sentence. Options A and D are misspelled. [Homonyms]

6. F *Be* is the correct answer. The homonym *bee* and option G do not make sense in the sentence, and option J is misspelled. [Homonyms]

7. B *Blew* is the correct answer. The homonym *blue* does not make sense in the sentence. Options A and D are misspelled. [Homonyms]

8. J *Die* is the correct answer. The homonym *dye*, which means "to color," does not make sense in the sentence. Option G does not make sense in the sentence, and option H is misspelled. [Homonyms]

9. A *Information* uses the most common "shun" ending, -*tion*. Options B, C, and D are spelled incorrectly. [Suffixes]

10. G The correct spelling of the number is *eight*. Option F is the homonym for *eight*. Options H and J are incorrect spellings. [Homonyms]

11. C The correct way to write the plural of *arena* is by adding an -*s*. Options A, B, and D are spelled incorrectly. [Plurals]

12. F In this context, the correct word is *won*. Option J is the homonym for *won*. Options G and H are spelled incorrectly. [Homonyms]

13. B The correct "shun" ending for *action* is the most common, -*tion*. Options A, C, and D are spelled incorrectly. [Suffixes]

14. J The plural of the word *sofa* is created by adding an -*s*. Options F, G, and H are spelled incorrectly. [Plurals]

15. A The correct "shun" ending for *session* is the second-most-common spelling, -*sion*. Options B, C, and D are spelled incorrectly. [Suffixes]

16. H The plural of the word *baseball* is made by adding an -*s*. Options F, G, and J are incorrect spellings. [Plurals]

17. B The correct "shun" ending for *position* is the most common, -*tion*. Options A, C, and D are spelled incorrectly. [Suffixes]

18. G The correct word choice for this sentence is *rode*. Option F is misspelled. Options H and J are homonyms for *rode*. [Homonyms]

Performance Assessment: Language

Sample Items (page 76)

A. D This option correctly uses the future tense verb form. The word *later* shows the event will happen in the future. Option A uses a present tense verb, but it needs a past tense verb. Option B switches verb tenses. Option C is missing a helping verb. [Verb Tense]

B. G This option uses the correct end mark: a period. Options F and H are missing end marks. Option J should end with a question mark. [End Marks]

C. A This option correctly joins the two subjects with the word *and*. Options B and D repeat the verb. Option C changes the meaning of the original sentences. [Sentence Combining]

D. H The first sentence is an asking sentence and needs to end with a question mark. The second sentence must start with a capital letter. Options F and G are missing capital letters at the start of the second sentence. Options F, G, and J have the wrong punctuation. [End Marks]

(page 77)

1 A The comparative *worse* correctly compares this year and last year. Option B is the adjective. Option C is the superlative. *Badder* is not a word (option D). [Adjectives]

2. H The sentence tells about something happening in the future. It needs the future tense verb form *will go*. Options F and J are past tense verbs. Option G needs a helping verb. [Verb Tense]

3. A The plural subject *girls* needs a plural verb: *cook*. Options B, C, and D are singular verbs. [Subject/Verb Agreement]

4. J This sentence needs a plural, object pronoun: *them*. Options F and G are singular pronouns. Options F and H are subject pronouns. [Pronouns]

5. C This option has both a subject and a predicate. The other options have subjects but are missing a predicate. [Sentence Recognition]

6. H This option has both a subject and a predicate. Option F is a predicate without a subject. Options G and J are subjects without predicates. [Sentence Recognition]

7. A This sentence joins the subjects with *and*, and it removes the repeated predicate. Options B and C change the meaning of the original sentences. Option D is too wordy, and it repeats the verb. [Sentence Combining]

8. G The sentence joins the three subjects and removes the repeated predicates. Options F and H are too wordy. Option J changes the meaning of the original sentences. [Sentence Combining]

9. B The sentence joins the objects without repeating the subject and verb. Option A repeats the subject and verb and changes the meaning of the original sentences. Options C and D are too wordy. [Sentence Combining]

10. J This sentence joins the predicates and removes the repeated subject. Option F repeats the subject. Options G and H change the meaning of the original sentences. [Sentence Combining]

11. B This sentence does not make sense in the paragraph. The other options are all about the same subject—getting a pet snake. [Supporting Sentences]

12. H This sentence does not make sense in the paragraph. The other options are all about the same subject—the new bed pillow. [Supporting Sentences]

13. D An asking sentence ends in a question mark. Also, Washington should be separated from DC with a comma. Options A and C have the wrong end marks. Option B begins a sentence with a lowercase letter. [End Marks]

14. F The first telling sentence ends with a period. The second sentence begins with a capital letter. [End Marks]

15. C Each important word in a proper name needs to begin with a capital letter. Linking words and articles do not need to start with a capital letter unless they are the first word in the title or name. Option A does not capitalize *museum*. Option B has an unnecessary comma after *Air*. Option D incorrectly uses a lowercase letter to start the word *air*. [Proper Nouns, Commas]

16 F The sentence needs a present tense verb. *It* is singular, so the verb should be singular, too: *isn't*. Options G and H are past tense. Options G and J are plural. [Subject/Verb Agreement]

17. B This sentence uses the correct plural subject pronoun and the correct end mark. Options A, C, and D all use object pronouns as subjects. Option C uses incorrect end punctuation. [Pronouns]

18. F The telling sentence needs a period at the end. Option G incorrectly uses an exclamation point. Option H uses a comma instead of an end mark to complete the first sentence. Option J uses the wrong end mark in the first sentence. [End Marks]

19. C The title of a work, such as a book, is capitalized. Use a capital letter to begin the title (*The*) and for important words in the title (*History* and *Flight*). The other options do not capitalize the title correctly. [Titles of Works]

20. G Use a comma between the date and year. Option F has an extra comma after *April*. Option H needs a capital letter to begin *April*. Option J is missing the comma between the date and year. [Commas, Letter Parts]

21. D Use a comma between a city and state. Option A is missing the comma. Option B has an unneeded comma after the state. Option C is missing the comma between city and state. It also has an unnecessary comma after the state. [Commas and City/State, Letter Parts]

22. G Proper names and titles begin with capital letters. Option F needs a capital *m* for *Mr*. Option H has an unnecessary comma after *Dear*. *Smith* is lowercase in option J. [Proper Nouns, Letter Parts]

23. A This sentence uses the singular subject form of the pronoun: *I*. Options B, C, and D all use object pronouns. [Pronouns]

24. H This sentence correctly uses commas in a series of three items. Option F has an extra comma after *and*. Option G is missing a comma after *lamp*. Option J is missing both commas. [Commas]

25. A Sentences that are statements end with periods. Option B uses a comma instead of an end mark. Option C uses the wrong end mark. Option D is missing an end mark. [End marks]

26. H This sentence uses commas to set off the name of the person directly addressed by the speaker. Option F places the second comma after *this*. Option G is missing a comma before the name. Option J is missing both commas. [Commas]

27. C These sentences tell about Mother cooking with apples. The other options do not support that main idea. [Topic Sentence]

28. J These sentences are all about Arturo training for a race. The other options do not support that main idea. [Topic Sentence]

29. A A comma is needed after *Susan* because the speaker is talking directly to Susan. [Commas]

30. H An exclamation point is needed after *Never* because it is a one-word sentence that shows a strong feeling. [End Marks]

31. C This asking sentence needs to end with a question mark. [End Marks]

32. J The sentence is punctuated correctly. [End Marks]

33. A A comma is missing after *City*. Use a comma between the proper names of cities and states. [Commas]

34. J The sentence uses the correct end mark. No other punctuation is needed. [End Marks]

35. D This part of the sentence does not need any changes. Option A is incorrect because a capital letter is needed to begin the sentence. Option B is incorrect because *Ours* is not the correct form of the possessive pronoun. Option C is incorrect because *They* does not make sense in the sentence. [Sentence Recognition, Pronouns]

36. F There should be no comma between the month and the day of the month. Options G, H, and J show incorrect comma placements. [Letter Parts]

37. C Proper nouns are capitalized. *Walnut St. Park* is the name of a specific park, so all the words in the name are capitalized. Options A, B, and D do not have all the words capitalized. [Proper Nouns]

38. G A comma is used to set off each of the items in a group. Option F includes an unnecessary comma after *dogs* and an unnecessary period. Option H is missing a comma after the word *ribs,* and it has an extra comma after the word *dogs.* Option J is missing two commas. [Commas]

(page 83)

39. A All words in the name of a street should have capital letters, even when one of the words is abbreviated: *Chestnut St.* Options B, C, and D have capitalization errors. [Proper Nouns]

40. H The first word of a sentence should begin with a capital letter. A phrase (or group of words) that introduces a sentence should end with a comma. Options F and J have capitalization and punctuation errors. Option G has a punctuation error. [First Words]

41. A This sentence explains why the writer is happy about the no-dog rule. Options B, C, and D are not about the pet rules that govern the writer's new place. [Unrelated Sentences]

42. J This sentence is another example of a strange law. It supports the topic sentence, and it makes sense with the other sentences. Options F, G, and H do not support the topic of strange laws. [Unrelated Sentences]

43. C It makes sense to sort through one's things before packing. Options A and D would fit better at the end of the paragraph. Option B should come at the beginning of the paragraph. [Sequence]

(page 84)

44. J This sentence explains why the men asked for more classes. Option F should appear earlier in the paragraph. Options G and H should come at the end of the paragraph. [Sequence]

45. A This sentence states the topic. It provides the context for the other sentences. Options B, C, and D do not belong in this passage. [Topic Sentence]

46. G A set of quotation marks is needed to close the quotation. Options F, H, and J are incorrect for this sentence. [Quotation Marks]

47. C A question mark should end an asking sentence. Options A, B, and D are not needed in this sentence. [End Marks]

48. G The beginning quotation mark is missing. Options F, H, and J are incorrect for this sentence. [Quotation Marks]

49. A The comma is missing after the beginning phrase that introduces the quotation. Options B, C, and D are incorrect for this sentence. [Commas]

(page 85)

50. F The singular possessive of *mouse* is mouse's. Options G, H, and J are incorrect for this sentence. [Apostrophes]

51. B The correct contraction for *did not* is *didn't.* Options A, C, and D are incorrect spellings of the contraction. [Apostrophes]

52. J The date is written correctly. There is a comma between the day and the year, and the month is capitalized. Options F, G, and H all have errors. [Letter Parts]

53. B Both words in the street name need to be capitalized. Options A, C, and D all have errors. [Letter Parts]

54. F A comma is needed between the city and state. Options G, H, and J all have incorrect punctuation. [Letter Parts]

55. C Both *dear* and the job title need to be capitalized. A colon follows the opening greeting in a business letter. Options A, B, and D are wrong. [Letter Parts]

Performance Assessment: Vocabulary

Sample Item (page 86)

A. C *Fresh* is used in this sentence to describe clean clothes. Options A, B, and D do not mean the same thing as *fresh.* [Synonyms]

1. D In the first sentence, *will* means "a legal paper read after someone dies." In the second sentence, *will* is used as a helping verb. Options A, B, and C each make sense in only one of the sentences. [Multimeaning Words]

2. F The word *point* correctly completes both sentences. Option G completes only the second sentence. Option F completes only the first sentence. Option J does not complete either sentence. [Multimeaning Words]

3. B The synonym for *improved* is *repaired.* Options A, C, and D do not have the same meaning as *improved.* [Synonyms]

4. J *Park* means "to leave" the car. The other options are not synonyms for *park.* [Synonyms]

5. A In this case, *wood* refers to the *boards.* Option B offers another meaning for the word *woods,* and options C and D are incorrect. [Synonyms]

6. G *Loud* is a synonym for *noisy.* Options F, H, and J are not synonyms for *noisy.* [Synonyms]

(page 87)

7. C Based on the context clue "has not been cut for three weeks," *long* is the word that makes the most sense in the sentence. [Words in Context]

8. J You buy groceries at a market, so option J is correct. A post office (option F), a museum (option G), and a library (option H) do not sell groceries. [Appropriate Word]

9. C People read books. You do not read muffins (option A), keys (option B), or trees (option D). [Appropriate Word]

10. F Based on the context clue *nurse,* *hospital* is the best answer. Options G, H, and J do not make sense in the sentence. [Words in Context]

11. A A baseball is *round,* so option A is correct. The other options do not describe a baseball. [Appropriate Word]

12. H A person who is *upset* is *sad.* Options G and J are the opposite of *upset.* Option F does not relate to *upset.* [Appropriate Word]

13. C The directions ask what musicians *do,* which indicates a verb is needed. Musicians *sing,* so option C is correct. The other options are nouns and do not name what musicians do. [Appropriate Word]

14. F Fish live in the water and need *fins* to swim. Fish do not have *fur* (option G). *Hooks* and *poles* (options H and J) are items used when people go fishing. [Appropriate Word]

(page 88)

15. B *Soap* is used to clean things, and it makes bubbles. The other options do not make sense. [Words in Context]

16. F The writer says the dog was washed outside, so only *yard* makes sense. The other options do not make sense because they are not places where dogs are washed. [Words in Context]

17. C The dog rolled around on the ground outside, so it makes sense that she would have *leaves* in her fur. The other options do not make sense. [Words in Context]

18. J Since the dog was dirty, the writer had to *wash* her again. The other options do not make sense. [Words in Context]

19. A *Oranges* can be purchased at the grocery store and used to make juice. The other options do not make sense. [Words in Context]

20. J *Money* is used to pay for items at a grocery store. The other options do not make sense. [Words in Context]

Performance Assessment: Language Mechanics

Sample Item (page 89)

A. A This asking sentence ends with a question mark. The other options are telling sentences and should end with periods. [End Marks]

1. A This sentence starts with a capital letter and ends with the correct end mark. It also uses capital letters to start the words in the proper name. Options B, C, and D should show capital letters for the following words: *University, Street,* and *Marie.* [First Word, End Marks]

2. H The sentence correctly begins with a capital letter and ends with a question mark. Option F needs a period at the end of the sentence. In option G, the name *sam* needs to be capitalized. Option J needs a question mark at the end of the sentence. [Proper Nouns, End Marks]

3. B This sentence starts with a capital letter and ends with the correct end mark. It also uses capital letters to start the first and important words in the title. Option A should capitalize the book title. Option C

should capitalize the words in the proper name *Ray's Ribs.* Option D should capitalize the title *My Boy.* [Titles of Works, End Marks]

4. F The sentence uses the correct end mark. The other options should end in periods. [End Marks]

5. A This sentence uses commas to set off Lori, who is being addressed directly. Options B, C, and D are missing the comma needed to set off the name. [Commas]

6. H This sentence starts with a capital letter and ends with the correct end mark. The other options are missing capital letters at the beginnings of the sentences. [First Word, End Marks]

(page 90)

7. B This sentence correctly uses commas in a list. Option A is missing a comma after *Maya.* Option C has an extra comma after *or.* Option D is missing a comma after *May.* [Commas]

8. F This sentence uses capital letters to start all of the words in a proper name. Option G should capitalize *music.* Option H should capitalize *school.* Option J should capitalize *street.* [Proper Nouns]

9. A The sentence correctly begins with a capital letter and ends with a question mark. Option B is incorrect because there is no question mark at end of the sentence. Option C is incorrect because *Her* should not be capitalized. Option D is incorrect because it should end with a period. [First Word, End Marks]

10. J This sentence correctly uses a comma to set off the opening word that modifies the words that follow. The other options are missing a comma between the opening word and the words they modify. [Commas]

11. B This sentence correctly uses commas to set off *Lucy.* Option A needs commas around *a good friend of ours.* Option C needs commas to set off *the purple ones.* Option D needs commas to set off *who is usually a good dog.* [Commas]

12. F This sentence correctly uses a comma before the word *so* to link the sentences. Option G uses the comma incorrectly after the linking word. Option H has an extra comma after the linking word. Option J has an unneeded comma after *sunny* and is missing a comma before the linking word *but.* [Commas]

13. B This sentence uses a comma between the name of a city and state. Options A and C are missing commas between the dates and years. Option D is missing a comma between the city and state. [City/State, Commas]

14. G In this case, the word *class* is singular. To form the singular possessive, add *'s: class's.* Options F and H are incorrect. Option J shows the plural possessive, which is used when more than one class is being described. [Apostrophes]

15. A This sentence requires the possessive form *its* rather than the contraction *it's* as shown in Option D. Options B and C are incorrect. [Apostrophes]

16. H To form the contraction of *would not,* remove the *o* in *not* and replace it with an apostrophe: *wouldn't.* Options F, G, and J are all misspelled words. [Apostrophes]

(page 91)

17. D The month is capitalized, and the day and the year are separated by a comma. Options A, B, and C are incorrect. [Proper Nouns, Letter Parts]

18. F Both the city and the state must be capitalized and separated by a comma. There is no comma between the state and the zip code. Options G, H, and J all have mistakes. [City/State, Letter Parts]

19. B The first word in the salutation of a letter is capitalized. Any names must be capitalized. The salutation is followed by a colon. Options A, C, and D are incorrect responses. [Proper Nouns, Letter Parts]

20. H The closing in a letter begins with a capital letter and ends with a comma. Only the first word in the closing is capitalized. Options F, G, and J all have errors. [Letter Parts]

Performance Assessment: Spelling

Sample Item (page 92)

A. C *Sleepy* and *meal* both have long *e* vowel sounds. Option A (*rain*) has a long *a* vowel sound. Option B (*pet*) has a short *e* vowel sound, and option D (*time*) has a long *i* vowel sound.

1. C *Sale* is the correct spelling for the selling of items. Option A refers to large pieces of cloth on a boat. Options B and D do not fit this sentence. [Long Vowels]

2. J *Read* is the correct spelling for a story. Option H is the color. Options F and G are the wrong words for this sentence. [Long Vowels]

3. B *Hi* is a greeting. Option A refers to the placement of an object. Option D means "to hurry." Option C is a misspelled word. [Long Vowels]

4. F *Close* means "to shut." Option G refers to items people wear. Options H and J are wrong words for this sentence. [Long Vowels]

(page 93)

5. A In this case, *general* is spelled with a soft *g.* Options B, C, and D are misspelled words. [R-controlled, Variant Spellings]

6. H Apple is the word that is spelled correctly and best fits in the sentence. [Double Letters]

7. A The *k* is silent in *knots.* Options B, C, and D are misspelled words. [Silent Letters]

8. J In the double *ll* combination in *hallway,* the second *l* is silent. Options F, G, and H are misspelled words. [Double Letters]

9. C *Asistant* is misspelled; the correct spelling is *assistant.* The other options are spelled correctly. [Double letter]

10. G *Nite* is misspelled; the correct spelling is *night.* The other options are spelled correctly. [Silent Letter]

11. A *Beelieve* is misspelled; the correct spelling is *believe.* The other options are spelled correctly. [Long vowel]

12. F *Aight* is misspelled; the correct spelling is *eight.* The other options are spelled correctly. [Long vowel]

(page 94)

13. A *Motion* is the correct spelling. The suffix *-tion* is the most common spelling for the sound *"shun."* Options B, C, and D are incorrect. [Similar Word Parts, Suffixes]

14. H *Television* is the correct spelling. The sound *"shun"* can be spelled *-sion.* Options F, G, and J are incorrect. [Similar Word Parts, Suffixes]

15. B *Wrinkle* is spelled correctly. Options A, C, and D are misspelled. [Variant Spelling]

16. F *Through* is spelled correctly and makes sense in the sentence. Option G is misspelled. Options H and J do not make sense in the sentence. [Silent Letters]

17. B *Shugar* is misspelled; the correct spelling is *sugar.* The other options are spelled correctly. [R-controlled]

18. G *Decisiones* is misspelled; the correct spelling is *decisions.* The other options are spelled correctly. [Inflectional Endings, Plurals]

19. A The correct answer is *ate.* The homonym *eight* does not make sense in the sentence. Options B and D are misspelled. [Homonyms]

20. J The correct answer is *Your.* The homonym *You're* does not make sense in the sentence. Option F is misspelled, and option G does not make sense in the sentence. [Homonyms]